LEARNING AIRPORT BUSINESS BEHAVIOR

JOHN LOK

2020 Jan. Print Published

Contents

Preface *vii*

Prologue *xi*

1. How Applying Economy Theories Solve Economic Problems 1

2. Airport Travellers Need Emotional Labor Sincere Service 66

3. Lean Maintenance Repair And Manual Error Airport Avoids Accident Service Occurrence Demand 75

4. Influencing Air Connectivity To Airport Environment Service Quality Demand 87

Preface

Introduction

What are our social customer and economic problems usually we will encounter in our lives. Can economists apply any economic theories to attempt to solve any economic or customer problems absolutely, such as traveller individual travelling package service choices? Whether can apply behavioral economic method to raise productivity, service performance in organizations and predict consumer individual emotion in consumption market.

Nowadays, travellers enjoy to go to different countries to travel. In consumer psychological view, instead of the travelling agents' travelling e-ticket cheap and fast seats online booking service or walk in travelling travel agents travelling paper ticket purchase or attractive trip arrangement service to attract travelling consumers' choice.

In any countries, whether attractive airport appearance design, airport convenient public transportaton tools service, e.g. enough airport bus, taxi, train, tram , underground train , ferry etc. number supplying , which can let any foreign travellers find and choose any kinds of public transportaton tools to catch to arrive destinations when they arrive any countries' airports easily, different kinds of varoety of attractive product shops or food courts/ shops which can let airport passengers to sit down and choose any kinds of food to eat or they can choose any books, magazines, or stationerys or cigarettes, wine, toys , electronic products, e.g. desktop, laptop computers etc. products to consume for reading or using need in the

airport's any restaurants or ships conveniently.
All these airports' intangible or tangible factors whether they can influence consumers' shopping desires in airports, even whether these both factors can attract or persuade many travellers prefer to choose to go to the country to travel and increase the country's travellers number. Concerning these two questions, my readers can earn more useful opinions to analyse whether any country's airport's image will have relationship to influence travellers' tourism choice and tourism consumption choice behavior , due to the country's airport's facility management , service, appearance design , convenient transportation, safety etc. important factors influence in order to assist to develop the country's tourism industry success in possible.
Does this travelling entertainment activities similar fee comparison factor influence any travellers choose to find the cheaper travelling entertainment activities arrangement provider? If travelling entertainment activities arrangement price is not the main factor to influence traveller individual choice. What other factors can influence traveller individual travelling entertainment activities arrangement choice? I shall explain what the other factors are influcenced traveller individual travelling entertainment arrangement choice.
The factors include that the cultural distance on satisfaction and travel intention factor, the lifestyle concept in travel behavioral factor, the business travellers motivation behavioral factor, the impacts of peer-to-peer accommodation use on travel patterns factor, factors influence local tourists decision-making be on choosing a destination factor, transportation, shopping centers, travelling destination facilities supplying factor, social media travelling networking sites promotion factor,

traveller's travelling experience psychological factor, travelling service for disabled people's travelling need factor, green travel entertainment service for environment protection travelling environment need factor the impact of travel blogging on the tourist, traveller individual vacation destination choice factor, economic impact to the traveller individual sudden changing factor.

I shall explain how and why any countries' airports shopping service provisions (service and shopping supply) which will influence overseas countries travellers' tourism choice to the country in preference (traveller individual airport service demand) in demand and supply economic theory view.

Prologue

Table of content

Chapter 1

How applying economy theories solve economic problems p.5-19

Demand And Supply Theory Solves Consumer Problems p.20 30

Consumer choice theory solves consumer problems p.31-43

Microeconomics Models and Theories solve customer problems p.44-61

Demand and supply theory solve social problem p.62-82

Chapter 2

Airport travellers need emotional labor service p.83-96

Chapter 3

Lean maintenance repair and manual error airport avoids accident service occurrence demand p.97-105

Chapter 4

Influencing air connectivity to airport environment service quality demand p.106-120

ONE

HOW APPLYING ECONOMY THEORIES SOLVE ECONOMIC PROBLEMS

The economic problem – sometimes called the basic or central economic problem – asserts that an economy's finite resources are insufficient to satisfy all human wants and needs. Economics involves the study of how to allocate resources in conditions of scarcity However, viewing economics as the study of how society allocates resources can lead to conflation of normative economic planning and empirical study of how economic agents operate in these conditions.

In mainstream neoclassical economics, it is assumed that humans pursue their self-interest, and that the market mechanism best satisfies the various wants different individuals might have. These wants are often divided into individual wants (which depend on the individual's preferences and purchasing power parity) and collective wants (which are the wants of entire groups of people). Things such as food and clothing can be classified as either wants or needs, depending on what type and how often a good is requested.

However, economists have sometimes characterized "how" to produce as a "technological problem" of efficiency whereas the allocation of what is produced is an "economic problem". In a free market, the "how" of production and allocation of resources is distributed among economic agents. In a centrally planned economy, a principal decides how and what to produce on behalf of agents. Modern economies are often welfare capitalist with various regulations, which makes the economic system more equitable while retaining the distributed free market system. Due to human wants are unlimited, an infinite series of human wants remains continue with human life. Nobody can claim that all of his wants have been satisfied and he has no need to satisfy any further want. Everybody feels hunger at a time then other he needs water. Sometime one feels the desire of clothing then starts to feel the desire of having good conveyance. When all existing wants are satisfied then new wants starts to create in mind, so the series of wants remains continue till the last moment of life. So an economic problem arises because of existence of unlimited human wants.

- Problem of allocation of resources

The problem of allocation of resources arises due to the scarcity of resources, and refers to the question of which wants should be satisfied and which should be left unsatisfied. In other words, what to produce and how much to produce. More production of a good implies more resources required for the production of that good, and resources are scarce. These two facts together mean that, if a society decides to increase production of some good, it has to withdraw some resources from the production of other goods. In other words, more production of a desired commodity can be made possible only by reducing the quantity of resources used in the production of other goods. The problem of allocation deals with the question of whether to produce capital goods or consumer goods. If the community decides to produce capital goods, resources must be withdrawn from the production of consumer goods. In the long run, however, [investment] in capital goods augments the production of consumer goods. Thus, both capital and consumer goods are important. The problem is determining the optimal production ratio between the two.

In fact, in our societies, resources are scarce and it is important to use them as efficiently as possible. Thus, it is essential to know if the production and distribution of national product made by an economy is maximally efficient. The production becomes efficient only if the productive resources are utilized in such a way that any reallocation does not produce more of one good without reducing the output of any other good. In other words, efficient distribution means that redistributing goods cannot make anyone better off without making someone else worse off. (See Pareto efficiency.) So, scientists will apply efficient distribution methods to help any countries to earn the absolute advantages when we buy and sell any kinds of products or food between ourselves countries, e.g.

when US has good natural resource to grow any food, e.g. potato, wheat , vegetable, cotton , then US can export to sell to China, because China has no any farms to grow agriculture food to supply itself Chinese to eat. So, China must need to buy any agriculture food from US. Otherwise, China has cheap labor to supply to US any manufacturers to help them to manufacture their electronic products. SO, it has many US factories are built in China to let Chinese workers help them to produce their products because their wages are cheaper to compare US workers. So, comparative economic advantage will be choice to apply between US and China both countries. (Absolute advantage trade theory)

The inefficiencies of production and distribution exist in all types of economies. The welfare of the people can be increased if these inefficiencies are ruled out. Some cost must be incurred to remove these inefficiencies. If the cost of removing these inefficiencies of production and distribution is more than the gain, then it is not worthwhile to remove them.

- The problem of full employment of resources

In view of how to use available resources are fully utilized is an important one. A community should achieve maximum satisfaction by using the scarce resources in the best possible manner—not wasting resources or using them inefficiently. There are two types of employment of resources:

(1) Labour-intensive

(2) Capital-intensive

In capitalist economies, however, available resources are not fully used. In times of depression, many people want to work but can't find employment. It supposes that the scarce resources are not fully utilized in a capitalistic economy.

- The problem of economic growth

If productive capacity grows, an economy can produce progressively more goods, which raises the standard of living. The increase in productive capacity of an economy is called economic growth. There are various factors affecting economic growth. The problems of economic growth have been discussed by numerous growth models, including the Harrod-Domar model, the neoclassical growth models of Solow and Swan, and the Cambridge growth models of Kaldor and Joan Robinson. This part of the economic problem is studied in the economies of development.

- Needs and wants problems

Needs are things or material items of peoples need for survival, such as food, clothing, housing, and water. Everyone has a different needs and wants. Until the Industrial Revolution, the vast majority of the world's population struggled for access to basic human needs.

Wants are effective desires for a particular product, or for something that can only be obtained by working for it. While the fundamental needs of survival are key in the function of the economy, wants are the driving force that stimulates demand for goods and services. To curb the economic problem, economists must classify the nature and different wants of consumers, as well as prioritize wants and organize production to satisfy as many wants as possible.

- Five bases problems of economy

In our societies , in general, our societies will have these similar problems The following points highlight the five basic problems of an economy. The problems are: 1. What to Produce and in What Quantities? 2. How to Produce these Goods? 3. For whom is the Goods Produced? 4. How

Efficiently are the Resources being utilized? 5. Is the Economy Growing?.

Problem 1:What to Produce and in What Quantities?

The first central problem of an economy is to decide what goods and services are to be produced and in what quantities. This involves allocation of scarce resources in relation to the composition of total output in the economy. Since resources are scarce, the society has to decide about the goods to be produced: wheat, cloth, roads, television, power, buildings, and so on. Once the nature of goods to be produced is decided, then their quantities are to be decided. How many tones of wheat, how many televisions, how many million of power, how many buildings, etc. Since the resources of the economy are scarce, the problem of the nature of goods and their quantities has to be decided on the basis of priorities or preferences of the society.

If the society gives priority to the production of more consumer goods now, it will have less in the future. A higher priority on capital goods implies less consumer goods now and more in the future. But since resources are scarce, if some goods are produced in larger quantities, some other goods will have to be produced in smaller quantities. Suppose the economy produces capital goods and consumer goods. In deciding the total output of the economy, the society has to choose that combination of capital goods and consumer goods which is in keeping with its resources.

Problem 2: How to Produce these Goods?

The next basic problem of an economy is to decide about the techniques or methods to be used in order to produce the required goods. This problem is primarily dependent upon the availability of resources within the economy. If land is available in abundance, it may have extensive cultivation. If land is scarce, intensive methods of cultivation may be used. If labour is in abundance, it may use labour- intensive techniques; while in the case of labour shortage, capital-intensive techniques may be used.

The technique to be used also depends upon the type and quantity of goods to be produced. For producing capital goods and large outputs, complicated and expensive machines and techniques are required. On the other hand, simple consumer goods and small outputs require small and less expensive machines and comparatively simple techniques.

Further, it has to be decided what goods and services are to be produced in the public sector and what goods and services in the private sector. But in choosing between different methods of production, those methods should be adopted which bring about an efficient allocation of resources and increase the overall productivity in the economy.

Problem 3. For whom is the Goods Produced?

The third basic problem to be decided is the allocation of goods among the members of the society. The allocation of basic consumer goods or necessities and luxuries comforts and among the household takes place on the basis of among the distribution of national income. Whosoever possesses the means to buy the goods may have then. A rich person may have a large share of the luxuries goods, and a poor person may have more quantities of the basic consumer goods he needs.

Problem 4: How Efficiently are the Resources being Utilised?

This is one of the important basic problems of an economy because having made the three earlier decisions, the society has to see whether the resources it owns are being utilized fully or not. In case the resources of the economy are lying idle, it has to find out ways and means to utilize them fully.

Problem 5: Is the Economy Growing?

The last and the most important problem is to find out whether the economy is growing through time or is it stagnant. If the economy is stagnant at any point inside the production possibility curve, it has to be moved on to the production possibility curve PP whereby the economy now produces larger quantities of consumer goods and capital goods. Economic growth takes place through a higher rate of capital formation which consists of replacing existing capital goods with new and more productive ones by adopting more efficient production techniques or through innovations.

All of these economy problems will be our societies often causes to anyone feels need to solve problems in order to achieve our societies can have enough resources to satisfy our every day living.

● The Consumer Problem

Consumer theory is concerned with how a rational consumer would make consumption decisions. What makes this problem worthy of separate study, apart from the general problem of choice theory, is its particular structure that allows us to derive economically meaningful results. The structure arises because the consumer's choice sets are assumed to be defined by certain prices and the consumer's income or wealth. The consumer's problem is to choose that is most preferred or, equivalently, that has the greatest utility.

The assumption of perfect information is built deeply into

the formulation of this choice problem, just as it is in the underlying choice theory. Some alternative models treat the consumer as rational but uncertain about the products, for example how a particular food will taste or a how well a cleaning product will perform. Some goods may be experience goods which the consumer can best learn about by trying ("experiencing") the good. In that case, the consumer might want to buy some now and decide later whether to buy more. That situation would need a different formulation. Similarly, if the agent thinks that high price goods are more likely to perform in a satisfactory way, that, too, would suggest quite a different formulation. Agents are price-takers. The agent takes prices p as known, fixed and exogenous. This assumption excludes things like searching for better prices or bargaining for a discount.

Hence , it seems that economic problems and consumer problems are similar, I feel that it is possible , economists can attempt to apply any economic theories to solve some consumer problems in some situations. They can find the accurate solutions when they can apply the suitable economic theories to solve the suitable consumer or economic problems in our societies. I shall indicate that how economists can apply the suitable economic theories to attempt to solve some consumer problems in our societies as below

Demand And Supply Theory Solves Consumer Problems

What is economy rule predict consumer behaviour? Why and How does economist can apply economy rule to predict consumer behaviours? I shall explain the reasons as below:

Why does economic principle be the best to predict consumer behaviour. It may include these two reasons: The first focuses on the substantive domain of study, in this interpretation , economics is a social science devoted to understanding how the economy works. The second definition focuses on methods: economics is a way of doing social science, using particular tools. In this interpretation the discipline is associated with formal modelling and statistical analysis rather than particular hypotheses or theories about the economy. Therefore, economic methods can be applied to many other areas besides the economy, everything from decisions within the family to questions about political institutions.

- Demand and supply principle predict public transport tool passenger behaviour

Economists need to use the right economic ideas to predict consumer behaviour. So, Misuse the wrong economy ideas to predict consumer behaviours. It will do more wrong judgement to evaluate or predict why and how and when the country's consumer behaviours will change. It is every economist needs to consider issue. For example, the economy idea application of economic supply-demand principles to public transport. Different fares would give commuters with more-flexible hours the incentive to avoid peak travel times. They would allow passenger traffic to spread out over time, reducing the pressure on the public transport system when enabling even larger total passenger flow. IT aims to reduce traffic congestion, increased public-transport use, reduced car-bon emissions and cause air pollution and generated considerable revenue for the country's transport system. So, if the country can apply supply and demand economic principle to attempt to predict how many passengers number needs to catch transport tools to go to work or go to school or other activities. Then, it can predict how many bus, ferry, taxi, train, underground train, tram etc. different public transport tools to satisfy future public transport passengers' needs in society. So, this demand and supply principle is the comparative best rule to predict any kinds of public transport passengers' road needs, when they need to either go to school, go to office, go to leisure or shopping etc. different kinds of activities. So, applying the demand and supply principle to predict road and sea public transport passengers can help the country to reduce air pollution when they feel that they can find any public transport tools to catch any time conveniently , then it can encourage them to reduce car purchase desire. When many people choose to catch public transport tools, then it will reduce many cars number on the road. Then, air pollution will reduce as well as any public transport tools' income will also increase as well as traffic jam will also reduce. When the country can evaluate how many people choose to catch bus or taxi or ferry or train or underground train, or tram or train etc. different kinds of public transport tools, then the country can predict the more accurate public transport tools number to every kind of public transport tool to satisfy their journey needs. e.g. whether underground train or train or tram need to decrease or increase the frequent times or number to catch the volume of passenger in busy or non-busy time; or whether bus company has need to increase how much buses to catch the city location passengers when they are living in the city. Moreover, supply and demand principle can help any public transport tools to explain why their passengers number reduces in the year, it may due to fare charge is unreasonable, feeling uncomfortable to sit on the seat or air condition is poor in the transport tool environment, or there are no more seats because many there are much time is full passenger and no seat vacancy to provide to them to sit . So, supply and demand principle can help any kinds of public transport tools to find whether which is (are) the factor(S) can influence the current or last year passengers number reduce. Then, they can concentrate on improving their weaknesses to raise their service quality . So, supply and demand principle can also help they to evaluate whether what their weakness are in order to improve to increase passengers number. They can do questionnaires to enquiry their passengers' response to evaluate whether which areas of services that they feel unsatisfactory. So, the different kinds of service satisfactory feeling to the passengers number data will be the main source to help the kind of public transport tool to analyse and conclude the results more accurate, then they can make the more accurate judgement to improve the of service. For example, the questionnaires indicate that the many passengers feel the bus fare is reasonable, but many passengers feel they can not find any seats to sit easily. So, it implies that the bus firm ought buy more buses or enlarges bus size and increases more seats in the enlarged buses. Then, it does not reduce its fare but it needs to find solutions to let passengers can find seats to sit in every bus more easily. But, if the questionnaires indicate that there are many passengers feel its fare is higher or unreasonable to compare other kinds of public transportation tools. Hence, it can avoid to spend more expenditure to increase bus number to the city, if the city has many passengers , they still choose bus to catch, but they feel its fare is too higher to compare other kinds of public transport tool. Then, it only needs to reduce its fare , it ought help it to increase passengers number. Hence, demand and supply principle is the most suitable economic method to evaluate any kinds of public transport system passenger needs in any country nowadays.

- Supply and demand and price elasticities principle predict oil energy user behaviour

The another case is that demand and supply principle can predict oil buyer behaviour to find whether what factors can cause the oil buyer individual need reduces. For example , a rise in production costs increases market prices and reduces quantities demanded and supplied. Or when, energy cost rise, utility bills increases and households fid extra ways of saving heating and electricity. But, others are nor. For example, whether a tax is imposed on the producers or consumer of a commodity, say oil has nothing to do with who ends up paying for it. The tax might be administered on oil companies, but it might be consumers who really pay for it through higher prices at the pump. Or the extra cost might be imposed on consumers in the form of a sale tax, but the oil companies might be forces to absorb it through lower prices. It all depends on the " price elasticities" of demand and supply. With the addition of extra assumption, this model also generates rather strong implications about how well markets work. In particular, a competitive market economy is efficient in the sense that it is impossible to improve one person's well-being without reducing somebody.

- Demand and supply principle can misuse to predict consumer behaviour when the two firms participate advertisement to promote their products in the same time

Why can demand and supply principle misuse to predict

consumer behaviour when the two firms participate advertisement to promote their products in the same time ? I shall explain as below: Assume that two competing firms must decide whether to have a big advertising budget. Advertising would allow one firm to steal some of the other's customers. But when they both advertise, the effects on customer demand cancel out. The firms end up having spent money needlessly.

We might expect that neither firm would choose to spend much on advertising, but the model shows that this logic is off base. When the firms make their choices independently and they care only about their own profits, each one has an incentive to advertise, regardless of what the other firm does. When the other firm does not advertise, you can steal customers from it if you do advertise, when the other firm does advertise, you have to advertise to prevent loss of customers. So, these two firms end up in a bad equilibrium in which both have to waste resources. This market can not apply demand and supply principle to predict consumer behaviours because they depends advertisement to promote their products. If these two firms advertise their products in the same time. Then , it is not possible that if one firm increases it price and it will cause its customer number loss, due to its advertise can help it to attract customers to consider its product from television or radio or newspapers or magazine promotion channels. So, I suppose that these two firms decide to increase their price, when they advertise their products to let customers to know in the same time. They will not lose their customers or reduce their customers easily. Because their customers can be persuaded to choose to buy their products to compare other similar products in preference. So, their increasing price will not influence their customers number lose easily. It explains that demand and supply principle is not right to this case, so demand and supply principle can misuse to help them to predict consumer behaviours when they advertise their products in the same time. Also, demand and supply principle is not suitable to them to predict consumer behaviours when they advertise their products in the same time. They will do wrong prediction to their consumers purchase desire when they advertise their products in the same time.

ON conclusion, using these demand and supply and price elasticity techniques, economists derive specific prediction for how consumers choose which products to buy, how households save, how firms invest, how workers search for jobs, as well as for how these actions depend on the particulars. They can help them to predict job and consumption behaviours more accurate, it depends on whether the situation is right, such as both competition firms participate to advertise their products in the same time case, it is not right to apply above economic principle to predict consumer behaviours. They will get wrong prediction when they apply this principle to predict consumer behaviours.

However, demand and supply principle can predict below any one of these cases. I shall indicate as below:

The problem of need-based scholarships: Most systems for providing college scholarships are based on some definition of financial needs, with scholarships generally being given only to those students who must need financial help in order to attend school.

Is need, rather than academic ability, the best basic on which to choose those students who are to be encouraged to attend college? Which way of choosing who gets aids is the more just? Which is the more efficient ? Is the overall educational level of society increased more by giving financial aid to bright students or to needy students? Presumably the aid offers more leverage to needy students, since they all need the money in order to attend college, whereas, many of the bright students would attend college in any case. But is a smaller number of bright students the more important addition?

So, the school can apply demand and supply principle to predict whether how many parents feel need financial assistance and evaluate how much financial amount is the right to borrow. It aims to calculate how many parents feel real financial need and how much to lend to them in order to let these students to get the most fair financial assistance. Assuming the school wish to use need as a basis, how does the school determines " financial need"?

Is need a function or parents' income? What, then , does the school about children of wealthy parents who are living independently of them and get no aid from parents? Should they be punished for their parents' wealth? But if they are given aid, won't all students, in order to get aid, claim to be independent of their parents?

Is need solely a matter of family income, or should not the school takes a family's financial obligations into account? Does not it make more sense to give aid to someone whose parents must put night more children through school than to someone from a family of five or one only with the same income? But in a possible parallel situations, should a family that carries mortgages on one or two large homes get preference simply because they do not have much money left to spend on college? Does doing this reward ? Is there a difference between the case of night children and the case of the large mortgage? How should parents who are not married , but are living together and supporting their children jointly be counted? Most parents are supporter to their children , although they are married in possible.

So, the school needs to gather all these data to evaluate how many parents are not married or married or living with their children together, how much salary they earn as well as every family has how much children as well as whether they have mortgage for their houses. So, these number will be the financial education assistance demanders, but it does not represent their real financial needs. It is possible that someone does not feel any financial need, although their children apply financial assistance to your school. Then , your school needs to evaluate whether how much financial assistance can lend to every real financial need student family. It can not exceed your final financial expenditure budget (supply) , when your financial expenditure is not enough. SO, demand and supply principle can be applied to research this school real family financial demand to lend to the real financial need families and evaluate whether the reasonable financial amount to lend to every child family to study in your school.

● Supply and demand principle applies to immigration to decide wage case

A fascinating and important example of supply and demand, full of complexities, is the role of immigration in determining wages. If you ask people , they are likely to tell you that immigration into California or Florida US, surely lowers the wages of people in those regions. It is just supply and demand analysis of immigration. According to this analysis, of these to these two regions in US. Immigration in to a region shifts the supply curve for labor to the right and pushes down wages. Why has it relationship between immigration to US these two regions immigrant number and wage?

Careful economic studies cast doubt on this simple proposition, however, a recent survey of the evidence concludes:

The effect of immigration on the labor market outcomes of natives is small in US. There is no evidence of economically significant reductions in native employment. Most analysis, finds that a 10 percent increase in the fraction of immigrants in the population reduced native wages by a most 1%.

How can we explain the small impact of immigration on wages? The main mistake is to forget how mobile the American population is and that the impact of immigration on wages, we must examine the effect of new immigrants when the strength of the local economy and the number of native-born residents in a city are unchanged, that is , when these other things are held constant. Unless you exclude the effects other changing variables, you can not accurately predict the impact of immigration. The same principle holds in doing a supply0and demand analysis of any market. As much as possible, when you are examining the impact of a supply or demand shift, you must try to keep all other things constant.

- Rationing by prices

By determining the equilibrium prices and quantities of all inputs and outputs, the market allocated or rations out the scare goods of the society among the possible uses. Who does the rationing? A planning board? Congress or the president? BO, the marketplace, through the interaction of supply and demand, doe the rationing. This is rationing by the purse.

What foods are produces? This is answered by the signals of

the market price. High oil prices stimulates oil production, whereas low food prices drive resources out of agriculture. Those who have the most dollars votes have the greatest influences on what goods are produced. All of these considers how demand and supply to the market.

For whom are goods produces? The power of the pursue indicates the distribution of income and consumption. Those with higher incomes end up with larger houses, more clothing, and linger vacations. When the most urgently felt needs get fulfilled through the demand curve.

Even, the how question is decided by supply and demand. When corn prices are low, it is not profitable for farmers to use expensive tractors and irrigation systems, and only the best land is cultivated. When oil prices are high, oil companies drill in deep offshore waters and employ novel seismic techniques to find oil.

IN sum , any thing needs through demands, interact with costs of goods, as reflected in supplies in our economic world. Hence, demand and supply theory ought be the most accurate method to help any businesses or governments to predict their shareholders behaviours when they will change as well as how and how their behaviours change.

Consumer choice theory solves consumer problems

What is 'consumer choice theory'?

'Consumer choice theory' is a hypothesis about why people buy things. Put simply, it says that you choose to buy the things that give you the greatest satisfaction, while keeping within your budget. At the heart of this theory are three assumptions about human nature.[1]

The first assumption is that when you shop, you choose to buy things based on calculated decisions about what will make you happiest. In economics language, this is known as utility maximisation (Economists really like to put quite simple concepts into long complicated terms.)

Secondly, the theory assumes that no matter how much you shop, you will never be completely satisfied. In other words, you will always be happier consuming a little bit more. This is known as the principle of non-satiation.

Thirdly, even though you always get more happiness from more consumption, the amount of pleasure you get from each good decreases with the more you consume. So if you eat two ice creams rather than one, you get more overall pleasure, but the second ice-cream won't be as satisfying as the first. This is known as decreasing marginal utility.

Consumer choice theory has influenced everything from government policy to corporate advertising to academia. But the theory has been criticized for not being the most accurate description of how people actually make choices. A whole new branch of economics, called 'behavioral economics', has emerged essentially to use findings from psychology to disprove the assumptions behind consumer choice theory. This has also led others to argue that consumer choice theory is less about describing how we do actually behave, and is more about describing how people should behave.[3] In other words, by portraying people as self-interested shopaholics, economists are saying that is it okay and natural for us to be avid consumers.

- Consumer choice theory can be applied to solve consumer problems during the country can have economic growth , the reasons may include as below:

The scenario leading to inflation starts with poor growth. Forget about everything that comes next and focus on that most important factor. Because it happens that the scenario leading to a budget crisis also starts with poor growth, and the scenario leading to a long-term unemployment crisis starts with poor growth, and a scenario leading to a better-the-neighbor trade crisis starts with poor growth, and so on. So a very important question is: what can be done to improve the prospects for economic growth? In particular, what is the right countercyclical approach to take to best situate the economy for future growth? I shall indicate during US, America's economy growth occurs, then economists can attempt to apply customer choice theory to solve US itself country's consumer problems more easier.

In no small part, the question comes down to interpretations of charts like the one at right. On the one hand, long and deep downturns seem to have almost no effect on the long-term rate of growth. On the other hand, in the long run we're all dead, and those who live during an extended period of economic weakness suffer for it. Meanwhile, it's also difficult to see where high debt levels influence the long-run rate of growth, at least where this chart is concerned.

During to the medium-term growth stage, is the bigger threat to American growth rates a market revolt against American debt levels? Or is it structural unemployment stemming from the slow, jobless recovery? Or is the cyclical shortfall in public investment? Or something else entirely? Of course, there's no real reason one has to choose a problem to address at the expense of others. More aggressive monetary expansion could make the finding of a solution to all these problems easier, but the Fed is unwilling to oblige me on this score. It may well be concerned that lack of fiscal discipline will lead to increasing inflation expectations, making its job harder (but then fiscal problems are trace able to growth). If that is the worry, however, one has to ask why the Congress has been unable to strike a deal for $20 billion in stimulus this year for $80 billion in fiscal tightening in a year or two (fill in whatever amounts you wish). But the outlook for the American economy vis-a-vis any number of potential crises will hinge on growth, and growth will hinge on the ability of private business to exploit promising opportunities as they arise. And the question is: what's likely to hurt that ability most? High interest rates? Lack of consumer demand? A shortage of adequately prepared workers? Right now firms appear to be most worried about demand shortfalls. So how much can you boost demand without making the primary fear high interest rates? A lot, if the expansion is on the monetary side.

● How to supply consumer choice theory to predict Consumer Behavior Marketing at Apple Computer

During US economy growth, Apply computer applies consumer choice theory to solve its computer buyers' choice problems among different kinds of brand computer competitors. Have you ever wondered why Apple is so successful? They were not the first company to invent the personal computer, portable music device, the tablet, the smartphone, software to download music, or the set-top box to name a few. Apple has amassed a brand loyal following like no other brand backed by significant sales, market share, and profitability. So, how does Apple do it? What's the secret behind their success?

Marketing using consumer behavior insight is how Apple succeeds. Even though Steve Jobs and Apple, did not use consumer research in the initial development of most products, consumer behavior plays a huge role in their marketing and ultimately the success of the company. Once a consumer purchases a product or downloads iTunes Apple has access to data the company leverages. Apple uses this information to gain significant insight into the consumer and what drives purchase behavior.

Consumer behavior marketing is an essential ingredient in the current business climate. The companies that apply this type of marketing well have a distinct competitive advantage that distances them from their rivals. Consumer behavior research is the primary driver at the core of any good strategy. Research provides actionable insight and ensures business success.

If you answer no to the following questions, this post is for you?

•Are you applying consumer behavior marketing currently?

•Have you conducted consumer behavior research within the last two years?

•Do you have consumer behavior marketing in your marketing plan with well-defined marketing strategies and tactics?

•Are you achieving the maximum results for your organization?

Every business has a target audience and consumer behavior marketing provides the fundamental methods for understanding your target. Consumer behavior research provides the underlying element that drives quality strategies and ensures business results.

"Marketing is understanding your buyers really, really well. Then creating valuable products, services, and information especially for them to help solve their problems."

The organizations that have an intimate understanding of their target audience possess a competitive advantage over those that do not. Establishing a one-to-one relationship and thorough knowledge of your target audience is a core

responsibility for business in the 21st century and beyond. Regardless if you are B2B, B2C, B2G or a hybrid organization you have a target audience. The information in this post can be applied to any business type. This post focuses on Apple (B2C) employing consumer behavior marketing as a critical ingredient for their success.
Hence, Apply computer shops have several computer teachers to teach any visitors how to use its laptops, hen they enquire its any computer salespeople. Due to its salespeople had been trained to learn how to use the different kinds of laptops. So, anyone enquires them, they can answer their enquires concern any computer questions immediately. Then, they will feel Apple laptops are the first choice to compare other kinds of laptops brands. It is one salespeople answering strategies to persuade any Apple computer visitors to feel its any laptops are the first or preference choice to compare its competitors in this computer market, so customer choice economic theory is the most suitable strategy to solve Apple computer's customer individual purchase decision problem.

Microeconomics Models and Theories solve customer problems

Microeconomics is concerned with the economic decisions and actions of individuals and firms. Within the broad church of microeconomics, there are different theories that certain assumptions and expectations of economic behaviour. The most important theory is neo-classical theory, which places emphasis on free-markets and the assumption individuals are rational and seek to maximise utility. However, there are many critiques of the neo-classical model, arguing economics is more complex with issues of market failure and irrational behaviour.

Pre-classical microeconomic theory

Before, Adam Smith, economics was more disparate with no commanding overall theory. Philosophers like Aristotle and Plato made references to issues in economics such as division of labour. The dominant ideas, pre-classical economics, were based on theories of mercantilism – the idea a nation should try to accumulate gold.

Classical microeconomic theory

Classical microeconomic theory was developed by Adam Smith (Wealth of Nations, 1776) and later economists, such as David Ricardo The essential aspect of classical microeconomic theory include:

Adam Smith mentioned the 'invisible hand of the market.' He noted how when people act out of self-interest, markets tend to provide goods and services which are demanded by the population. It needed no central price setting, but market forces responded to changes in demand and supply, e.g. a shortage pushes up the price and causes demand to fall.

Smith also investigated topics such as the division of labour, specialisation and economies of scale. The early classical economists emphasised the importance of costs to firms and consumers.

Utility maximisation

An important development of classical economics towards the end of the nineteenth century is the concept of utility maximisation. The concept of utility was developed by philosophers/economists – Jeremy Bentham and John Stuart Mill. In microeconomic theory, it was believed a consumer will buy goods depending on the marginal utility (satisfaction) they get from the good. This theory assumes consumers are rational and seeking to maximise the satisfaction they get.

Neo-classical theory

Neo-classical theory is a modern re-interpretation of classical economics of the nineteenth century. Neo-classical theory places importance on markets, but developed new ideas, especially regarding utility and rational choice theory. Elements of neo-classical theory.

1. Market distribution of goods and services.
2.R ational choice theory. This is the idea individuals hold rational preferences and make rational choices; seeking to maximise their outcomes – be it profit, wages, consumption or investment.
3. People act independently and make use of available information.
4. Marginalism. In neo-classical economics, more emphasis was placed on concepts of marginal utility and marginal cost. We make choices depending on satisfaction we get from one extra unit of a good.

Economists such as Carl Menger, William Stanley Jevons and Marie-Esprit-Léon Walras. and Alfred Marshall developed ideas such as diminishing marginal utility. Many of these neo-classical economic theories were brought together in Alfred Marshall's very influential textbook, Principles of Economics. (1890)

·Note there is some blurring between classical economics and neo-classical economics.

·Neo-classical economics has also come to mean 'orthodox economic theory. To a large extent, it has incorporated new developments in microeconomics, such as theories of market failure, market structure and econometrics.

Theories of Market failure

Neo-classical economics has become associated with a belief in the efficiency of markets. However, microeconomic theory has also incorporated the criticisms and limitations of free-markets.

·Monopoly. Adam Smith was well aware of the problem of monopolies and how firms could use their market power to set excessive prices.

·Imperfect competition. In the 1930s, Joan Robinson developed a model of imperfect competition, an awareness many markets were somewhere between monopoly and perfect competition often assumed in neo-classical economics.

·Externalities. Developed by Arthur C.Pigou in The Economics of Welfare (1920) this is the awareness production and consumption decisions can have harmful (or positive) effects on third parties. Therefore, a free market can lead to overconsumption of demerit goods and negative externalities.

·Game theory. An awareness, decisions are not linear or simple, but the interdependence of agents influences what we decide to do.

Behavioural economics

The most important trend in recent decades in economics is the greater emphasis placed on aspects of behavioural economics, which uses many insights from related fields such as psychology.

·Disputes rational choice theory. The essential element of behavioural economics is that it argues individual agents are often not rational and often do not seek to maximise utility.

·Behavioural economics examines how agents can be influenced by biases, and make decisions not predicted by neo-classical economic theory. Behavioural economics can explain the irrational exuberance of booms and busts.

Econometrics

In the post-war period, economics became increasingly mathematical with economists attempting to use mathematics to explain models and theories. Econometrics looks at economic data and seeks to extract simple relationships. The basic tool is the linear regression models and can be used to try and predict consumer spending and demand for labour.

Heterodox models of microeconomics

Heterodox models differ substantially from microeconomic foundations of neo-classical economics. Schools of thought include

Marxist economic theory

Karl Marx developed an alternative perspective on economics. He focused on the surplus value created under the capitalist economic system. To Marx, the invisible hand of the market would be better described as the invisible hand of capitalist exploitation of workers. Marx claimed workers did receive their full labour value but were compensated for their necessary labour only – enabling capitalists to profit from the surplus.

Institutional economics. The role of society and institutions in shaping economic behaviour. For example, Thomas Veblen looked at theories of 'conspicuous consumption' and noted how the desire for social status could drive much economic theory. Institutional economics could be seen as a forerunner for later behavioural economics.

Environmental economics Argues traditional economics wrongly places value on increasing output. The most important thing is creating a sustainable environment which maximises living standards. So, manufacturers need to consider how to manufacture their products , but pollution can not be raised as the same time, because human will face to raise cost of living and living

experiences to be poor , even food shortage, water pollution , air pollution , death rate raises when technological productivities brings pollution to our natural environment. Hence, environmental economoic theory is the most suitable to solve manufacturers' pollution problem.
Buddhist economics/non-profit goals. Like environmental economics, this questions the assumption higher incomes and higher output are desirable. The theory of hedonistic relativism suggests higher incomes do nothing to increase happiness levels, and traditional economics can encourage society to pursue materialistic goals which actually create more problems of stress, conflict and environmental degradation.
Some of the basic models you might find in A-Level economics :

- Price Discrimination
- Perfect competition
- Price Mechanism
- Monopoly
- Oligopoly and kinked demand curve
- Game Theory Pricing strategies
- Market failure
- Behavioural economics

ON conclusion, any macro economy theories can be applied to find the most reasonable methods to solve any customer problems in societies by economists as above. So, I believe that any economic and customer and social problems can be solved by economic theories in our society.

Demand and supply theory solves social problems

Over the past 20 years, many researchers believe to apply behavioral economic macroeconomic models which can predict market behavioral change. The reasons are based on assumptions of optimizing behavior in many cases have difficulty accounting for key real-world observations. Hence, researchers have used behavioral economics assumptions with the aim of making their model predicting better fit the data. The reason for behavioral economics results into macroeconomics will be more accurate to predict market behavioral change in macro-economy view point, such as economic fluctuation prediction, the consumption, formation of expectations and determination of wages and employment how to aggregation supply and the possibility of consumer individual demand product or service number prediction more accurately.

- How to apply behavioral economy (demand and supply) theory to predict marketing behavioral changes more accurate?

Anyway, economists aim to develop models of human behavior and interactions in market in order to build useful models. Economists make simplifying assumptions to analyze why the market will be changed by consumer individual consumption behavior changing.

Why do I assume consumers are as economic man ? In behavioral economy view point, how the perception of the economic man's behavior (including consumer choices) of economic models with the development of economics as a science. Economists explain the concept of economics as a science. It is the concept of consumer as an economic man, the essence and complexity of consumer behavior.

The consumer and consumer purchasing behavior are an important area of interest of many scientific disciplines. The process of economic decision making as well as consumption choices are connected with wider human activities. The terms of both consumer individual attitudes and group social behavior will influence group social behavior will influence consumer individual final consumption decision in every consumption choice process. Thus, behavioral economy method can predict consumer behavioral changing, it can apply these sciences to research, includes sociology, psychology, anthropology, operational research, decision theory etc. different literature research aspects. I assume that businessmen can apply behavioral economy method to predict market changing behaviors successfully if they own behavioral economy knowledge.

In this part, I shall concentrate on explain how the perception of the economic man's behavior (including consumer choice) is applied to predict market behaviors. After explaining the concept of consumer as an economic man, the nature and complexity of consumer behavior are discussed to below different industries' marketing behavioral changing every case studies in US or UK countries.

Why is consumer as an economic man? IN behavioral economy view point, the concept of answer is one of the fundamental concepts in economics because the consumer is the case market participant along with the producer. In general, lecturers define the consumer in various ways, but in behavioral economy view point, consumers mean economy man. Because who will compare cost and benefit to any product or service to decide to choose to buy the product or consume the service. Consumers are as "economic man", who will make own subjective preferences (tastes), habits and traditions and existing objective constraints (i.e. disposal income) market prices of products and services in order to satisfy whose needs to a maximum degree and in the most rational way.

Thus, economic man means consumers need to make psychological mind to decide whether who either prefer to buy this product or another product or prefer to consume this service or another service more suitable. Thus, any markets or industries need have themselves benefits and consumers must need to evaluate whether the product or service has more benefits to compare other products or services in the consumption market to satisfy whose needs. It means that if the product or service has more benefits to compare other similar products or services. Then the product or service will persuade many consumers to choose to but the product or consume the service.

Consequently, in first part, I shall indicate how to apply behavioral economy theory : economic man psychological method, benefits and costs benefits method, how to predict these US and UK enterprises marketing behavioral changing more accurate.

In the second part, I shall apply micro employee behavioral economy concept to explain how to solve these US and UK inter-organizational management challenge.

I believe that behavioral economy method can be applied to research organizational employee behaviors change, e.g. how any why the employee chooses to do this action in whose organization. Moreover, behavioral economy method can be applied to consumption market to predict how any why the consumer choose to buy the product or consume the service. So, any consumers and employees personal psychology and external environment economic factor will influence how to choose to do decision in any organizations or consumption environment.

Bibliography

Bandiera, O., I. Barankay, and I. Rasul (2005). Social preferences and the response to incentives: Evidence from personal data. The quarterly journal of economics 120 (3), 917-969.

Exadaktylos, F., A.M. Espin and P. Branas-Garza (2013). Experimental subjects are not different. Scientific reports 3, 1213.

Lazear, E.P. (1979). Why is there mandatory retirement? Journal of political economy 87(6), 1261-1284.

● Behavioral economic method (demand and supply theory) predicts stable basic income consumer individual spending behavior

Can apply behavioral economic method to predict that the consequences of a stable basic income consumer's consumption behavior? It may be significantly different than the ones are predicted by the standard economic model if more realistic assumptions of human consumption behavioral prediction success.
Behavioral economic method assumes that consumer will compare whether whose benefits are more than costs after they buy the product or consume the service. I assume the consumer is only the who have stable basic income source consumer target. This stable basic income target consumers who will evaluate or feel they will earn more benefits than costs to every product in their consumption process, after they will make final decision to choose to buy the product to use or consume the service. Otherwise, if they feel they won't earn more benefits after they buy the product or consume the service in the consumption process. Then, they won't choose to buy the product to use or consume the service. In behavioral economic view point, it indicates their consumption behaviors are depend on comparing the

product or the service whether it can satisfy their desire benefits and their desire benefits to the product or service must be more than their consumption cost.

There are four points to apply behavioral economic method to predict each stable basic income individual income spending. They include: motivation, conspicuous consumption, social preferences and crowding theory.

Each stable basic income consumer individual spending amount will be different and it is represent that every high stable basic income consumer must decide to consume any high cost services or buy high cost products to use. Although some economic teachers assume general high income people will accept to spend more expenditures for enjoyment or buy high cost of products to satisfy basic high level necessary expenditures. But, applying behavioral economic analysis, it is not absolute true, some low income people also accept to spend more to buy high cost of products or increasing spending expenditures for enjoyment for their basic necessary expenditures.

The field of behavioral economic can be fined as a combination of economics and psychology that tries to capture human behavior in a more realistic. Understanding each consumer individual consumption behavior, we need to know how who does each decision to influence each consumption choice. Consequently, analysis reaches the conclusion. Every high or low level stable basic income consumer individual behavioral consumption that the microeconomic consequences of a stable basic income of individual consumer target consumption group could be efficiency enhancing, but at the same time incentives about positional concerns could lead to wasteful and inefficient spending to the stable low basic income consumer target group.

- How to apply demand and supply theory to contribute to the stable basic income target consumer group's consumption prediction?

What is basic income mean? A basic income is an income paid by a political community to all its members on an individual basis, without means test or work requirement. How to apply behavioral economic method to contribute to the basic income consumption prediction?

I assume high incomc tax is charged to one high income tax payee , it will influence the high income tax payee individual consumption desires to be fallen, also extrinsic incentives will effort and intrinsic motivation and how the labor market change these variables under and big changes predicting, how income security changes social consumption preferences, e.g. how a big change affects the overall level of status -seeking behavior and this effect with income inequality to influence consumer individual consumption attitude or habit.

How can behavioral economic methods predict consumer's consumption decision, in special the stable basic income consumer target group? In any consumption decisions are involving risk and uncertainty, the standard economic model usually assumes that decisions are based on final condition, regardless of the changes are caused by the results of a consumer's decision.

An alterative mode of how consumers make decision and judgement under risk and uncertainty. This situation is often occurred in consumption market.

In behavioral economic view point, it explains how consumer's consumption, however, which excludes the stable basic income earn factor can influence the stable basic income earn target consumer group decides to make final consumption decision to compare to the non-stable basic income earn target consumer group. The reasons include as below:

(1) Consumers evaluate decisions over gains and losses with respect to some natural reference point, when they feel need to consume, which is assumed to be judgement about a sequence of outcomes are based on changes in wealth, rather than whether how much absolute basic income earn to influence whose consumption desires.

(2) Thus, behavioral economic theory assumes the consumer is the low level of income group in society, but when who feels that he is still gains more than losses when who decides to buy the expensive product or consumes the expensive service. Then, the low level of income consumer who will accept to buy the expensive product or consume the service easily. Due to whose gains feeling is more than losses feeling, when who buys the product or consumes the service.

(3) Behavioral economic theory also assumes the taxpayer will pay high income tax in this year. The, even the high income taxpayer can earn high basic income, but due to whom needs to pay high income tax in this year. Then, he/she will reduce much spending, even he/she reduces spending on cheap products or cheap service consumption for enjoyment. This is the taxpayer's economic decision to influence whose consumption behavior, due to the high income tax expenditure factor influences whose consumption behavior to change to be reduced spending expenditures in this year.

How to apply behavioral economic method to predict labor market changing behavior?

Instead of applying behavioral economic method to predict every consumer individual consumption effort. Behavioral economic method can be also be applied to predict every country's labor market changing behavior. Particularly, how salary clerical workers or low wage labor workers should move from one type of job to another based on these factors. They include as below:

Their intrinsic motivation and how their levels of effort would change after this movement, investigates the effects of income security on social preferences in labor market changing behavior, and how cooperation in social contribution is affected when income security is guaranteed, how to predict the role of positional externalities on conspicuous consumption and how would change the incentive to influence consumption. So, it seems that general labor market job changing behaviors will not influenced by external economic environment better or worse changing factor, or salary changing factor etc. different environmental condition changing factors influence to employees' job changing. Generally, employee's job changing behavior is more influenced to persuade who changes job by himself/herself intrinsic motivation negative emotion influence mainly.

How to apply motivation crowding theory to predict labor productivity? One of the main challenges of economic theory is to find what are the optimal incentives that increase productivity of labors. The standing point is usually extrinsic incentive be it is form of monetary compensations for high effort or fine for low effort.

It is a kind method of reward or punishment to increase or decrease number of productivity to every labor. But it can only raise short term number of productivity in possible and it can not guarantee high quality of productivity. So if one employer wants a labor to do more of an activity or with a higher quality, consider paying the labor for working hard on punishing whom if for providing a low level effort. This idea is that people do not like to work, and therefore they used some sort of compensation for doing a specific activity, and that the more they are paid the harder, they will work. So, payment better compensation is only beneficial to encourage labors to do one specific task or activity in short term. This method can not be suitable to rise long term beneficial productivity and high level quality of production or excellent performance in long term and it can only keep in short term raising productivity and high level quality of production or excellent performance benefits.

Consider paying the labor for working hard on punishing whom if for providing a low level effort. This idea is that people do not like to work, and therefore they used some sort of compensation for doing a specific activity, and that the more they are paid the harder they will work. So, payment better compensation is only beneficial to encourage labors to do one specific task or activity in short term. This method can not be suitable to raise long them beneficial productivity and high quality of products.

However, economists would argue that, is a labor has high intrinsic motivative to perform a task, who will provide a high level of effort without compensation by himself/ herself but an even higher level of effort of whom is compensated. If a labor does not have any intrinsic motivation to perform a task or an activity, who will provide no effort or a low effort of whom. There is no compensation, but who will increase this level of effort of an extrinsic incentive is implemented.

Hence, in behavioral economic view point, the labor

individual high level effort is a main psychological factor to influence whose productivity to be raised or the qualities of products to be raised, when the products are manufactured by the high level effort labor. It means that high compensation is not the good method to encourage labor productivity or raise quality. Otherwise, how to influence the one low level of effort of labor to change to be one high level of effort labor. It is the best psychological method to influence the labor to raise productivity and quality and service performance to any products or services in manufacturing process or service process for any organizations in long term beneficial possible.

● How can apply demand and supply theory raises basic stable income consumer consumption desire

Economists aim to develop models of human behavior and interactions in consumption markets. But consumers behave in complex ways, such as how to predict consumers to make rational decisions in consumption processes. Moreover, self-consumption control and motivation can vary significantly across different individual consumer.

In order to build useful consumption prediction models, economists make simplifying assumptions, aims to predict how to raise stable basic income consumer target group consumption more success. However, behavioral economy method is one kind of accurate consumption prediction method. It can be applied to predict economic decision-making to every consumer consumption choice more accurate raising whose consumption desire?

I shall indicate how to apply different behavioral economy methods (demand and supply theory) to raise stable basic stable income target consumer group consumption desire in these different consumption situation (consumption environment) aspects as below:

1. Stable basic stable income consumer group consumption great or small amount desire

The consumption of products and services is a fundamental part of consumer's welfare. Basically, every one who has stable basic stable income, who will like to consume any products and services. Even, consumption great or small amount desire won't be depended on whether the person whose income is more or less. It means low income level of people will still like to consume great amount to buy expensive products or consume expensive services, because consumption is human's part of life and basic needs.

This stable basic income people will like to consume, because they have stable income source when they do not worry about unemployment occurrence to cause them have no enough money to support their life. Otherwise, non-stable basic stable income people won't like to consume because they feel they have no stable basic income source to support their life and they will worry about unemployment occurrence any time. Hence, stable basic income people will have more consumption desire to compare non-stable basic stable income people in any countries usually. Behavioral economic method indicates they feel their economic benefits will be loss if they planned to buy any products or consume any services easily. So, they prefer to save money in bank more than consumption.

1. Demand systems and micro-economic factor influence basic income people consumption attitude

Why stable basic income people will like to consume? Because who have more demand, a demand system shows the level of consumer demand for different products and services: e.g. one basic stable income person may refer to the demand for clothes, another the demand for food etc. How the demand for that particular product varies with the prices and demographic factor will influence who to accept consumption. Such as stable basic income people who will not consider to decide to buy the cloth to wear or the food to eat if who feel the cloth or food price is even more expensive to compare other kind of cloth or food.

Otherwise, non-stable basic income people who will consider to decide to buy the cloth to wear or the food to eat if they feel that they still have enough cloths to wear or enough food to eat at homes , even these food or cloth price are less expensive to compare others. Because they feel they lack stable income effort to support them to consume. Hence, basic stable income factor can influence the consumer's consumption decision.

2. Life-cycle advertisement method can influence consumer individual consumption behaviors to be increased

Consumer behavior makes strong assumptions about the informational and computational bases of consumer behavior. Generally, consumer behavior is reasonably characterized as the maximization of expected lifetime utility subject to budget constraint and conditional on the available information.

Generally, consumers prefer to buy any discounted products or it is reasonable that consumers accept to buy many attractions to persuade them to buy any kinds of bargain discount products. Hence, low bargain discount product is one good behavioral economic principle to encourage or persuade or attract any consumers to increase consumption.

What is behavioral life-cycle model? This model explains consumer behavior can be persuaded to buy any discounted products by advertisement, e.g. television, radio, newspapers, magazine etc. promotion channels. Because frequent advertisement promotion method can let any consumers often remember the product's brand, discounted price, style, color and image from advertisement content.

So, advertisement can be one part of consumer behavioral life-cycle. For example, when the television audiences often watch TV. Hence, when the brand of product advertisement often makes fun image and discounted message to let TV audiences to remember this brand of product, when they are watching TV. Then, it has possible to persuade any potential consumers to choose to buy this brand of any products or consume this brand of any services, due to its advertisement of discounted sale message is very attractive to every one to let this advertisement audience's attention to remember this brand of products or services are selling or serving in market at this moment. So, it is advertisement image behavior influences audiences to buy the brand's any products attractively and persuasively.

3. Raising electricity consumption from electricity user individual habit

For electricity use market case example, how to analyze people's behavior in consuming electricity using a behavioral economic framework ? Electricity consumption is modeled by the means of consumer's individual useful habit, electricity price, consumer satisfaction level, willingness to invest in new technologies, social interactions, and marketing strategies by the power utility. Because electricity is necessary to every home or electric vehicle users needs or businessmen office etc. different needs every day.

Power companies supply electricity to a region's homes and industries. However, electricity needs modernization of power system companies expect to increase price. Due to competitive factor, such as other fuel resource choices, outdated kind of energy electricity supply, and renewable fuel energy source competition.

Hence, applying behavioral economic concept, I assume electricity consumers will compare to electricity and other kinds of energy choices to weigh up the costs and benefits of all alternatives, aiming to maximize their benefits, before making a decision to choose to use electricity for their house electricity demand or electric vehicle or shop or factory manufacturing etc. function of different aspects of electricity users.

For example, electricity business clients, they aim to reduce cost, such as energy expenditure, when they use any energy to manufacture their products in factories. If they feel electricity is expensive price to compare other kinds of energy power supply. When, they feel that they can not earn much beneficial advantages to use electricity to produce their products. Otherwise, if they feel other any kinds of energy supply can replace electricity to give more benefits to compare electricity energy. Then, many business electricity users will change to use other kinds of energies to consume to replace electricity power.

However, electricity can have competitive ability in electric vehicles market, if many drivers feel environment protection is more important to compare vehicles will be popular to be driven, due to many drivers don't want air pollution. They will like gas vehicles. Hence, the main attribute from the consumer side is one their habit electricity consumption behaviors, satisfaction level, energy efficient interaction with the power utility.

Consequently how to predict electricity consumer's demand. The important factor is how to let electricity users to feel power companies are changing a reasonable level to compare other similar energy supply products. When electricity users feel electricity which can bring more benefits to compare other kinds of energy products. Then, in energy supply market, if the demanding number of electricity consumers can increase more than other kinds of energy demanding number. Then, it is right time to raise electricity price to charge electricity consumers. Hence, how to persuade electricity consumers to feel that they can have more benefits to compare other kinds of energy products. It is the main successful factor to electricity power supply companies.

- Consumer confidence is as a predictor of consumption spending

Behavioral economists believe it has link between confidence and economic decisions to cause consumers to choose spending, if the consumer has confidence to believe the product is worth to use, then who will accept to buy the product to use.

Concentrated on the conceptualization of confidence and its role in mode in theories of consumption. It also concerns on whether the confidence indicators contain any information beyond economic fundamentals. The concern is whether confidence can be explained by current and past value of variables, such as income, unemployment, inflation or consumption or in other way.

Whether confidence measures have any statistical significance in predicting economic outcomes once information from the above variables is used. Economic variable factor will also influence consumer confidence to decide consumption spending, e.g. real consumption expenditures (income, wealth or interest rate).

Finally, it will identify under which circumstances confidence indicates can be a good predictor of household consumption. Hence, survey is one good measurement method to predict whether how much every household has confidence to spend to consume the brand of products to use. Why is survey a good confidence consumption measurement prediction to every household in every country?

The reasons include survey can gather every household consumption habit history data to evaluate whether every survey person has how much confidence to consume the brand of products. Which in most cases correspond to periods where there are large changes in household survey indicators, liking during financial crises or geopolitical tensions to measure or predict whether the country's future good or bad economic condition factor will influence every household consumption desire in the year.

This modelling approach assumes that there is a certain (unknown) in confidence index changes beyond which confidence starts impacting consumption behaviors. So, sample household surveys can show the contribution of confidence in explaining consumption expenditures increases when household survey indicators feature large changes. So that confidence indicators can have some increasing predictive power during the survey investigation period in the year.

Other view point, surveys have been concerned on whether the confidence indicators contain any information beyond economic fundaments. The concern is whether confidence can be explained by current and past values of variables, such as income, unemployment, inflation or consumption or the other way. Whether confidence measures have any statistical significance in predicting economic outcomes once information from different external variable factors to influence the survey household group.

What is confidence in consumption survey ?

Confidence in consumption. For example, to measure whether how much degree of strong inflation in the economy, such as recessions and recoveries will influence the country's household confident consumption in the year. The surveys consumers' questions usually concern on major expenditures and changes in the respondent's financial situation, focus on job availability and current business conditions etc. questions. It is then possible that about consumer confidence depending on the relative performance of the variables that may be more relevant balances, with respect to the factors that determine unemployment and other labor market related issues. It aims to investigate whether those any one of variable factors will influence consumers general loss confident consumption desire in this year.

What is a confidence indicator ?

A confidence indicator is considered as an explanatory variable for consumption together with standard variables used on predicting consumption expenditure. However, the natural real personal consumption expenditure is unexpected and unpredicted easily.

In conclusion, consumption expenditure depends the consumer individual confidence. If the consumer has much confidence to feel this year economic change will be better and he/she is easily to find job, then he/she will accept consumption easily in this year. It seems financial wealth and unemployment etc. economic factors will influence every household consumption desire. So, survey is one kind of good psychological consumption prediction method to predict consumption spending for any country in the year. I recommend manufacturers may choose to apply survey method to attempt to enquire sample survey people to gather data to predict whether what degree of consumption desire to them and find solution methods to solve low degree of consumption desire challenge.

How to apply behavioral economy methods to influence employee individual psychology to achieve raise productivity of long term incentive intention?

Increasing salary is short term incentive productivity method. Behavioral economy assumes labors will choose to do beneficial behaviors to themselves when they feel their work behaviors can earn more benefits to themselves more than their employers in the organizations. Otherwise, if they feel their work behaviors can earn more benefits to their employers more than themselves. Then, they won't choose to do their work behaviors, e.g. raising productivities or work hard. Due to they feel work hard or raise productivities behaviors that only give more benefits to their employers more themselves.

Whether does cheap product price incentive consumption desire to influence effective consumption behavior? Whether is monetary increasing salary payment incentive labors might be willing to work on task? I feel raising labors productivities is similar to raise incentive consumption, which both have similar point, such as increasing salary payment or cheap product price is the main factor to influence incentive consumption or raising productivities. Hence, it seems monetary factor is not the main effort to encourage labors to work hard.

In labor's behavioral economic view point, for example, if

an employer pays an employee more doing a task, who might be less willing to work on it, who might be less productive given whose efforts and who may enjoy the task less. If you want your employees to save more for retirement. You may want to give them fewer investment options. If you want them to engage more in a task, you might want offer them an additional alternative, instead of increasing salary to that task. Thus, increasing salary is not only method to encourage productivities of incentives.

How to improve the design of incentive structures to encourage productivities in any organizations?
Any monetary incentive can only encourage productivities in short term. It can not only encourage productivities in long term in any organizations. It is similar to cheap or discount product price can only attractive consumers to buy the product in short term, it can not attract consumers to choose to buy the product in long term, it prefers to have more options to encourage labors to incentive productivities, e.g. investing good beneficial retirement plans. Suggesting that employees do not have free disposal of their investment options. These standard incentives seem irrelevant raising salary monetary factor, they can be quite effective in inducing labors to take particular actions to incentive productivities in long term. Due to when they can hard work, then they have more beneficial retirement plans or investing plans for their retirement. It means when they can achieve the most effective or efficient productivities to the employer for long term. It will give better retirement benefits and investment benefits to the better or even the best performance of employees. Otherwise, the worst performance employees won't earn good retirement benefits and investment benefits, when their employers feel their perform very poor in the

organizations in long term.
Hence, increasing salary level method is not one successful long term incentive method to persuade every employee to raise productivities or encourage excellent performance optional method. Increasing salary level is only similar to reduce product price and it is only short term encouragement to consumption or productivities method.
In conclusion, extrinsic monetary factor can not incentive labor's raising productivities more than every employee themselves intrinsic motivation to raise productivities as excellent performance in any organizations. Thus, organizations need to let employees to feel that they can give long term economic benefits to encourage their intrinsic motivation effort to be raised their productivities or performance more effective or efficient in order to achieve long term both win-win economic benefits to employees and employers both.

Building employees and managers kindly co-operational relationship method

If you are an economist, your employer has no without any financial incentive to encourage your economic research tasks in your organization. It is equally difficult to certify that such activity will contribute to your growth of human capital and increased productivity in research or teaching.
The standard model, which explains employee's effort only through the way (determined by productivity), is therefore incomplete. In particular, it doesn't consider that incentives to work do not have to be monetary in other words, that there are other things besides the disutility of labor (Kamenica, 2012) and section 1.3 have.
Why will short term wage increasing method only influence short term labor supply to raise productivities? The effect of reference raising wage can be most easily

identified on short term labor supply to raise productivities. For US, New York city taxi drivers case, they have to decide every day for low long they are going to offer their services, given the day-to-day variable ability of demand they face (peaking during bad weather and/or when big conferences and public events are taking place in the city).

In the standard model, houses worked should grow with any growth in demand for New York taxi drivers' services. (one day's earning will have only a negligible income effect in the longer run). And yet actual cabbies work less on a demand heavy day. One of possible explanations suggests that New York city taxi drivers expect a certain income, they have set themselves a specific target income, who expect to achieve every day. During low demand for their taxi services, then they work longer hours to reach the target, when during peak demand, their referential income is achieved quickly and they only work short hours. Elasticity of hours worked with respect to their earnings is therefore negative (Lamerer, Babcock, Loewenstein, & Thaler, 1997).

However, taxi driver is either one self employment business or one taxi company employment driving service occupation. It is similar to other kinds of service jobs in societies. Servicing employees, such as waiters, salespeople, securities, customer services, bus drivers etc. different kinds of service occupations. They are not similar to manufacturing occupation to be applied how many amount of piece of products production to evaluate their productivities efforts. Thus these any one of service job nature is depended on their service performance to clients to feel their service performances are excellent to compare general service performance effort of service employees.

Considerably, respectively, I assume that if these service

employees' managers can build kindly working environment, e.g. manager individual attitude and behavior can let their employees to feel happy to work together in their teams. Then, the managers' kindly as enthusiastic behaviors or attitudes will let every employee more positive encouragement of service attitude to serve their clients in their teams. Then, the client complaining number will be possible reduced, even none of any complains. Hence, building kindly relationship between managers and employees will raise excellent service performance to any organization service nature employees.

Can bonus method encourage service performance to be raised ?

In service job nature of bonus method can also raise employees' overall productivities or service performance. For example, when employees got a provisional bonus before the start of the workweek, but were warned that they would lose it on payday, unless they achieve the productivities or excellent service performance norm, they worked more productivities or let many clients to satisfy their service performance. Hence, managers can achieve bonus plan to compensate any excellent productivity or excellent services to them. Then, they can let clients to feel their service performance more satisfactory than employees of a control group who were merely given the standard promise to receive a bonus upon achieving the norm.

The effort was relatively small, however, productivity grew 1%. Interestingly, the effect of a loss was stronger when how teams were rewarded this way, social pressure came to bear on the less productivity team members. When the team members won't earn any bonus. So, long-term productivity gains were achieved through bonuses paid by excellent performance compensation method to compare to low service performance employees receiving no bonuses at all.

Economic views of human motivation nature

There are only two main types of economic actors and by making simplifying assumptions about how these types of actors behave and interact. The two basic sets of actors in this model are firms, which are assumed in this model are firms, which are assumed to maximize their profits from producing and selling products and services, households, which are assumed to maximize their utility (or satisfaction) from consuming products and services.

It seems any employees will choose to do behaviors to achieve to earn much benefits from their organizations. The models of economic behaviors that consider considerate employees' choice of goals, the actions they take to achieve these goals and the limitations and influences that affect their choices and actions.

For university students choose which universities to study case, suppose that any college enrollment students are deciding which courses to study. Thus, it implies that if the university can provide many different kinds of suitable or right courses to any college enrollment students to choose to study. It means that if the university can provide many different kinds of courses to enrollment students to choose to study. Then, it will have much chance to attract enrollment students to choose this university to study. It's competition can be raised by many courses choice factor. but, in fact, it is not absolute right, although the university can provide many courses to provide to enrollment students to choose to study. But, it is not guarantee to represent it must attract many students to enroll this university to study.

For example, suppose that college enrollment students are

deciding which courses to choose to study. Although, it has right course to prepare to these enrollment students to choose to study. But, they see a summary of evaluations from hundreds of other students indicating that a certain course is very good in this university. Then, suppose that they match a video interview of just one student to give a negative review of this university of the course. Even when students were told in advance that such a negative review was worse to this university of the course. They tended to be more influenced by the negative review than the summary of hundreds of evaluations, even although such behavior seems irrational. Hence, although many right courses choice has much chance to attract students to enroll this university to study. But, if its bad educational quality from this course from negative review factor, which will influence the enrollment students number to be reduced.

It implies that students will compare this university's the course educational quality whether is better or worse to compare other universities' similar course educational quality, even this university's this course fee whether is reasonable in educational market. This is cost and beneficial comparison behavioral economy principle to all enrollment students before they decide to choose which universities.

Hence, this case implies that universities how to train teachers' teaching skills to let students to feel that they can learn new knowledge from their teaching staffs absolutely. It means how to raise education training skills to raise teachers' teaching performance. It is very important factor to influence the university's teaching development success. So, many courses choice is not important factor to attract many students to enroll the university. Otherwise, although the university can not provide many courses to let students to enroll, but it's teachers can provide excellent teaching service to teach whose students. This is important factor to attract many students to choose to enroll this university to study.

Under-level productive efficiency and low-consumption desire behavioral economic influences

In behavioral economic influence view point, I feel that under-level productive efficiency is the represent low production number to the manufacturer as well as low-consumption desire is not represent less consumers demands or customers lose confidence to the product.

On the one hand, I shall apply behavioral economic method to analyze why under productive efficiency is not represent low production number influence. Otherwise, I feel under-productive efficiency will have possible to increase production number after the manufacturer can review what factor(s) to influence under-productive efficiency.

I shall give reasons to explain as below:

As Jim, P. & Brendan. M. (2013) indicated who had ever been experiencing failure to do their businesses. Although, they had lost a million dollars, but they felt that they can be taught to learn undiscovered knowledge to know how to do their businesses successful by their wrong judgement and decision learning experience. They explained that " in ll risk taking, speculation, business ventures, entrepreneurial activities, it is the loss side on which you must focus first. This is even true for gambling, the gambler determines how much he's willing to bet, and loss, before the game is played. He doesn't wait for the game to end and then let the croupier or dealer assign his wager for him. How do you determine the downside, and how do you control or minimize it? With objective decision making and a plan that has as its starting point the stop-loss parameters"

Hence, it explains any business will have under-level productive efficiencies and low consumption desire business risk. However, to any one entrepreneur, who needs to know it is one game between the himself/herself and whose clients. They also need to know with objective decision making and a plan that has as its starting point.

Hence, I assume that if the entrepreneur has wrong decision to cause under-level productive efficiency, it is possible that, due to there is no enough employee number to manufacture the product or many employees are not skillful to manufacture all product in normal time or many employees are lazy etc. different factors to cause under-level productivities. However, when they discover their productivities are very low to compare similar competitors their employees' productivities and efficiencies. Then, they can attempt to find what factor(s) to cause low productivities and low efficiencies. it is possible that any one among of these factors case. They include many employees' lazy to influence low productivities or there is no enough employee number or many employees are not skillful to manufacture their products in production process.

Hence, wrong decision or plan is not represent failure. Otherwise, it can give chance to let the entrepreneur to learn whether what the factor(s) is (are) to cause low productivities and low efficiencies in whose product manufacturing process. As I feel that under-level productive efficiency is not represent low production number. Because I assume that if one worker lacks enough skills and manufacturing experiences to manufacture the product, but who can spend less time to manufacture the product and whose spending manufacturing time is same to the another owning enough skillful worker's time to do the product. Hence, I believe that the product quality from the low-skillful worker's manufacturing skill, it's quality will be worse to compare to the product quality from the high skillful worker's manufacturing skill. Hence, if the low skillful worker needs to spend much time to produce the product, but the product quality can be same to the high skillful worker's product quality. It means that it is sure because the low skillful worker has no excellent skill to compare to the high skillful worker to produce the product. Hence, his manufacturing spending time must be longer than the high skillful worker's time. It implies that the low skillful worker spends less time to raises high production number, but his product must be poor quality to sell. Then, his fast and efficient manufacturing speed that is not achieve economic beneficial to the organization's manufacturing process, e.g. less electricity spends to manufacture the product. Otherwise, the low skillful worker's fast and efficient manufacturing speed of behavior will raise the organization's cost in manufacturing process because consumers would not like to choose to buy any low quality product when they can choose which similar products to compare which one has the best quality and cheap price to buy.

Hence, efficient production is not the main factor to influence the business's success. Otherwise, good quality of the product factor is more important to compare it to influence the business's success.

On the other hand, I shall apply behavioral economic theory to analyze why low-consumption desire is not represent consumer demand lose to the business. As Jim. P. & Brendan. M. (2013) also identified " rather than looking for success to follow, who explained the formula for failure to avoid. As an Wang, founder of Wang laboratories said

" it is my belief that there are no secret to success." The formula for failure is not lack of knowledge, brains, skills or hard work and it's not lack of luck, it's personalizing losses, especially of preceded by a string of wins or profits. It's refusing to acknowledge and accept the reality of a loss when it starts to occur because to so so would reflect negatively on you."

Thus, as whose feeling to explain why low-consumption desire is not represent less consumers demands or customers lose confidence to the product. The reasons include the causes of low-consumption desire are possible due to worse economic environment factor influences consumption desire to be reduced. It is not due to whether the product price is too high or quality is worse to compare others. Hence, as Jim & Brendan indicated the formula for business failure is not lack of knowledge, brains, skills or hard work and it's not lack of luck. It's not lack of luck. It's personalizing losses, means its reflecting to knowledge and accept the reality of a loss when it starts to occur. As it is applied to explain why low-consumption desire is not represent less consumers demands or customers lose confidence to the product. It's possible that external economic environment changing worse factor to cause the business personalizing losses, it is not reflect who lacks knowledge, skill, hard work factors to cause failure. Hence, ho to predict when and how and why economic environment changes worse will be important factor to predict when and how and why consumption behavioral changes to cause business's success.

- Demand and supply theory solves organizational problems

Any organizations can let salespeople feel happy to sell their products. Then their sale performance will also raise. The question concerns that how to make them to feel happy to help the organization to sell their products? I shall explain some methods as below:

How to manage sales for predictable revenue? In order to hold salespeople sale psychology whether they feel happy or unhappy, executives need to understand the essential activities, sales managers must focus on to be analysts for change, foster continuous improvement and create a sales culture that drives results. Sale executives need to know how to achieve top objectives of sales management is to drive sales, capture new revenue and exceed monthly sales and margin objectives, e.g. performing sale strargy development with each salesperson on Monday morning at a minimum, and in a formal one-on-one meeting during the week;using strategy tools and questioning techniques to ensure the prospects are qualified and the strategy is valid; knowing the ratio between future values and future monthly quotos to raise sale opportunities; six month on-going sale plan aims to make sure there are coordinated to achieve sale to various market segments; developing on ongoing series of networking events to build market awareness in order to ensure all salespeople attend specific events involved in networking by salespeople to, understanding the market how to influence salespeople sale method to sale number, understanding trends and seeking some channels to raise additional sales opportunities; how to create trained or warm sale environment to let sales teams feel happy to sell.

How to design and utilize efficient control sale procedures? The sale cycle procedure may include these market activities, such as advertising, sales promotion, market research, physical distribution, pricing , sale place, sale staffs seeking. SO, any organizations need have good sale planning, direction and control of the personnel, selling activities of a business with including recruiting, selecting, training, rating, supervising, paying or reward system, motivating strategy , as all these tasks apply to the personnel sales-force.

The factors may influence salespeople psychology, they may include fair income reward system, or appreciation methods and sale career development plan to every salesperson. It aims to encourage them to achieve the highest sale effort. Anymore, methods to train sale managers have the right direction to guide, lead and motivate their salespeople, e.g. knowledge of salespeople psychology needs how to satisfy them, understanding why they choose to do or act themselves sale behaviors in order to improve their weakness to motivate salespeople to achieve company's sale target goal every month easily, e.g. raising profitability, sales volume, market share, growth and corporate image building raise clients' confidence to choose to buy this company's any products more easily.

The sales organization is required for the following purposes, they may include: enabling top-management, to devote to more time in policy making for the growth and expansion of business to divide and fix authority among the subordinates , so that they may shirk work, to avoid repetition of duties and functions, so that there may not be any confusion among them to locate responsibility of each and every employee , so that they can complete the whole work in stipulated time, if not then the particular person must be responsible, to establish the sales effort to enforce proper supervision of sales force.

What does the concept of salespeople replacement value mean? What is a sales force turnover management tool? Sales force turnover is defined as the rate at which salespeople leave an organizations, resignations, retirements or dismissals. So, if the organization can raise the sales force turnover ratio, because many salespeople can be promoted or the retirement, or the sales force turnover ratio raising reasons as well as they are not resignation or dismissal reasons. I believe that the organization ought have good sale environment and reasonable reward and welfare strategy to let its salespeople feel happy to help this company to sell its products every day.

However, sales management's actions have direct or indirect effects to impact on turnover. Direct effects may include the firm's firing or dismiss policy. The indirect effects on sale turnover may include new salesperon recruiting and selecting policies affect the quality and performance of the sale force as well as the speed at which salespeople are replaced. The same policies have an impact on the sales force turnover rate through the characteristics of the newly recurited salespersons and the promotion , training, retraining policies, support, supervision, compensation. ALl of those factors have an impact on salesperson's personal satisfaction or dissatisfaction absolutely. So, any sale organizations need to concern how and why whether any one of above these factors may influence their salespeople how to perform or act sale behaviors in order to excite their sale number more effective in long term.

How to achieve sale force management effectively? Sale management is one strategy to many organizations, because organizations expect their salespeople can only raise product sale number. So , they will consider whetther how to implement the sale management strategy to be the most suitable to themselves sale organizations in order to excite their sale teams to sell their products to achieve sale growth aim effectively. So for organization's long term sale growth development, it seems that one excellent sale management strategy can help the organization has stable sale number growth in long term possible.

However, the term " selling" includes a variety of sales situations and activities. For example, those sales positions where the sales representative is required primarily to deliver the product to the customer on a regular or periodic basis. The emphasis is this type of sales activity is very different to the sales position where the sales representative is dealing with sales of capital equipment to industrial purchasers. IN additions some sales representatives deal only in export markets whereas others sell direct to customers in their homes. So, sale organizations need to sell to local or overseas market as well as its target customer is businessmen or individual consumer or both in order to implement to choose their most suitable sale management strategy to train their salespeople more effective or achieving sale growth objective only. Because these its sale major target and where sale market place both factors will influence how it ought train its salespeople, so any organization's training method ought be influenced to change by whom is its major sale target and where is its major sale market location factors.

How to know the psychology of salesmanship? WHen the organization can predict or find reasons to explain why its salespeople feel unhappy to help

this organization to sell its products. Then, it can attempt to improve its weaknesses in order to let its salespeople to feel more sale service satisfactory feeling to continue to help this organization to sell its products. THen, it won't need not often to train or recruit new salespeople to replace its old salespeople in consequence. How to know what its salespeoples' real need in order to raise their sale service satisfactory feeling ?

Psychology means that " science of the mind" and psychology plays to important part in business and it is quite worth to bring to influence any organization salespeoples' posivitive or negative sale emotion in their every sale process between themselves and their every client in personal. For example, if the salesperson often have negative emotion or he feels unhappy in every sale process, then he will encounter or increase many times of sale failure possibilities. He will feel that he is one poor verbal advertiser or seller or promotor to help his organization to promote its products to sell again as well as he will lose confidence to sell any products next sale chance, because his failure sale experiences are accumulated to influence his sale emotion to be poor or difficult sale.

Hence, the poor performance salesperson needs have more successful sale experiences to compensate his / her prior many sale failure times feeling, if the organization hopes this poor performance salesperson can raise sale number easily. Overall, any organizations need to concern how to improve or raise the more failure times of sale experience salespeoples' sale techniques or methods or attitudes more than choose to fire or dismiss them as well as finding another new salesperson to replace him/her. Because it is possible that the salesperson 's poor sale performance that is not due to himself/herself poor sale effort and sale knowledge or lacking sale experience to the product, it may be due to the poor sale team cooperation relationship , feeling poor or not comfortable sale physcial shop environment, poor sale manager and other salespeople working relationship, the sale manager lacks leadership effort, poor family relationship etc. external factors more than himself/herself personal poor or negative emotion or poor health etc. personal factors. Hence, the organization ought enquire him/her why he/she feels unhappy to sell its products and it needs to attempt to find methods to solve his/her challenges immediately. If his/her challenges can be solved. It is possible that his/her sale efforts can be also raised for. So, if the organization can know how to utilize positive sale emotion psychological methods to predict or know why and how every salesperson perform his/her sale behavior in whose daily sale tasks, then it can concentrate on implementing effective and the most suitable sale training to raise their sale abilities more easily.

However, the sale training may include: How to build or improve long term good salesperson and his/her customer sale service relationship between every salesperson and every client in every buying and selling cycle process, how to using right communicating styleds for better understanding every client's real needs, powers and negotiating, e.g. every salesperson needs to review why there are many clients do not choose to buy any products from his sale presentation or promotion, finding every time sale failure reasons can let the salesperson makes himself/herself sale failure reasons evaluation or judgement in order to find what is the major reason influences his/her sale failure, e.g. lacking product knowledge, he/she often let many clients to feel that he lacks patience to listen the client's enquiry or feedback, his sale presentation is not attractive to let many clients like to stay longer time to listen his sale presentation in whole sale process, the salesperson himself/herself emotion is negative and he /she can let many clients feel he / she is not happy or does not enjoy to sell this product from himself/herself face impression or sale behavior impression easily, lacking enough sale techniques to persuade his/her clients why he/ she ought choose to buy this product in whole sale process etc. these factors may influence the salesperson's sale failure chance to be raised. Hence sales manager ought need to spend long time to meet the poor sale performance salesperson to discuess what his/her sale challenges are the most major to influence his/her every sale successful chance in order to improve his/ her sale performance more successfully.

IN conclusion, the reasons why salespeople often encounter sale failure possibilities. The factors may include these aspects, such as they lask the desire to help customers to make satisfactory purchase decisons, they only concern how to achieve sale final objective or aim only, it will cause clients feel they do not real concern their real needs. They only concern to sell the product in success. They do not know how to describe the product whether what characteristics or features it owns accurately in order to increase sale chance to persudade them to make final decision to by the product, they do not attempt to participate the whole sale process to help them to choose the most right product in order to satisfy their any purcahse needs, they ought avoid deceptive or manipulative influence tactics, avoid the use of high pressure sales techniques etc. Thus, if any organizations can spend time to investigate what factors cause why any one of salespeople choose perform his/her sale behavior often in order to know or understand their salespeople' sale psychology absolutely. Then, I believe that their sale number will only grown more easily.

TWO

AIRPORT TRAVELLERS NEED EMOTIONAL LABOR SINCERE SERVICE

Why does airport any service labour individual emotion (the airport any kinds of service labor his/her service provision) will influence any countries' travellers their preference airport staying choice (transfer air plane) and travelling destination preference choice(staying airport traveller individual service demand to airport service) in demand and supply view? Airline service industry, front line travelling passengers service workers' emotional challenge concerns cabin crew and airline ground service employee whose service quality or performance how to serve travelling passengers in order to reach service level or satisfy their service performance needs to be accepted. So, how to influence airline service labour individual emotional matter which will be one major factor to let travelling passengers how they feel satisfactory to the airline service.

The question concerns how to let airline service cabin crews and air ground service employees build long term good emotion to serve their airline travelling passengers. Because
bad emotional airline service labors will damage the whole airline employers' loyalty as well as reducing travelling passengers number in possible.

Will a lot stresses at work cause bad emotion to airline ground service employees? The hospitality industry comprises of travel and tourism and the major segments include lodgings and cuisines (hotels, restaurants), transport(airlines, rentals, cruise and railway companies), travel and tour operators. All of these related travelling industries' employees , they are emotional labor, whose service performance or service attitude will influence future potential travelling passengers' airline choices to the airline operating servicer again. Any airline service employees in these service sector industries, have to interact with their travelling clients, be its customers on a regular emotion reflecting basis. So, they must be patient to listen any travelling passengers' enquires in order to help them to solve any problems considerably.

Emotional labor is managing one's feelings to generate a publicly accepted facial and bodily display of emotion. Emotional labor is an expression of emotion for a wage. Jobs involve face to face or voice to voice interactions with clients (travelling passengers), jobs demanding the employee to produce and alter an emotional state in other person, and jobs allowing the employer to implement certain amount of control over the emotional activities of the employees, produce or create emotional labor among the employees.

Thus, long time bad emotional airline front labors number increasing, it will influence the airline whole service member performance to be its airline passengers. However, many airline organizations have their owning set of norms or policies that determine these feeling rules. These are specially seen in customer service industries. IN long term, these strict policies will let airline front service staffs feel stress or pressure, because they won't feel to be punished in possible, e.g. without salary continue increasing, dismissal (lose jobs), changing to another position to do more simple or boring job duties, if they are discovered that their working service performances are not satisfied to their airline employers in any time.

So, strict airline organizational policies will be one strict or pressure emotional regulation to any airline front service staffs. This emotional regulation refers to a person's capability to accept and understand his or her experience of emotions to get involved in healthy strategies in managing emotions which are uncomfortable whenever required, when they need to contact their airline passengers every day. In fact, it has possible that they will accept unreasonable complaint from their airline passengers, even they perform very good or they have help their airline passengers to solve any enquiries when they feel any needs, they stay in airports any time. So, it has close relationship among airline front service staffs' emotions and the airline's policy as well as their service attitude. Thus, good airline policy will build good airline service staffs' emotions and good service attitude or service behaviour to serve their airline passengers every day in possible.

Any airline organizations can not neglect to consider how to build (keep) good airline front labor emotion issue. Because they are any airlines' representatives, if they can build good

images to let the airline the airline passengers to feel. Then, it will influence many airline passengers to choose to buy the airline tickets to replace other airlines because they like its front airline front staffs' services. SO, any airline organizations need to consider front service staffs' health status and definite psychological or mental diseases more than physical diseases, because many airline front service staffs only need to serve their airline passengers and they do not need to move any heavy things in airports in general. They need to spend more time to contract their passengers more than any things. When their passengers give their passports or/and any related travelling documents, e.g. air tickets to them to check in to find whether they can allow to enter airport restrict areas, and if they give their luggage to them, they also need to help them to measure its size and weight heavy to decide whether they need to pay extra fee and their luggage are permitted either to keep to them together to enter the air planes to fly or separate air planes to fly to destination. So, they need to make accurate judgement need to avoid any error occurrence. They do not allow to do any wrong judgement or error in order to be complain by their airline passengers often. Hence, any airline organizations need have good method to help their airline front service staffs to avoid to do any wrong judgements in order to influence any flights delay or customers' complaints , due to their personal wrong judgement to their passengers cause in possible.

Thus, any airline organizations require to enquire themselves these questions: Is there any influence of emotional labor (surface acting and deep acting) on the general mental health or psychological disease of airline employees? Is these any difference in the experience of emotional labor across demographics (age/gender/mental status/work experience of airline employees influence their service performance? Because above any one factors , such as every airline front service staff individual age, airline service experience, marital status of these factors will influence their emotions to be good or bad to serve their airline passengers every day. Hence , any airline organizations need to investigate every airline front service employee individual background in order to arrange the most suitable policy to train their front line or ground airline service staffs' skill in order to let them to feel less stress or pressure

or they can feel happy to enjoy to serve their airline passengers.

On conclusion, reducing airline front or ground service staffs' psychological stress or mental pressure issue which will be the most effective or the best solution to assist them to raise confidence to serve their airline passengers in airports in long time. I believe that it is the most rapid psychological solution method to assist any one airline front or ground service staff to raise service level in short time.

● Airports service environment factor (staying the country airport traveller individual service and shopping demand to the country's airport)

The environment of airports service environment for the airline services, which will also influence travelling passengers' travelling destinations and travelling frequent times choices. The airport price factor includes income growth, aviation technology and local economic / geographical features of the country's domestic or overseas airports both. IN fact, airports, airports are indeed two sides businesses, it has commercial relationship between both airlines and passengers. So, airports' pricing will influence passengers' travelling demands to the airlines in the country. Any countries' airport(s) need(s) to respond how to help themselves country airlines how to increase passengers number and airlines choices in order to achieve attracting traffic on frequent air planes flying aim. Because the country's travelling passengers number increases , it will influence the country's airport(s) ' income increases indirectly, instead of the countries' any airlines themselves incomes.

Hence, any country's airport(s) will be one good platform to let travelling passengers to stay in the country's airport(s). It means that id the country's airport(s) can build good service image and reasonable products sale price and comfortable shopping environment to attract any countries' passengers feel comfortable and worth to stay in themselves countries' airport(s), when they need to transfer air planes to stay in the country's airport, e.g. one hour to five hours short time, even overnight long time staying. However, if they

feel the country's airport(s) are(is) more comfortable and clean to stay, less noise, as well as they have enough chairs to let them to sit or sleep and large area to let them to work in the airport ground floor.

Moreover, the country's airport(s) can have enough restaurants , bookshops, any electronic or other kinds product shop[s, even cinema etc. shopping or

entertainment services to satisfy
the passengers whose eating needs, entertainment needs, shopping needs in the airport. Then, I believe that the country's airport(s) can help itself airlines to attract many passengers
to choose to increase travelling times to the country frequently. For example, when the country's airport passengers feel that the airport restaurant food concessionaires will probably provide enjoy positive external gains from having more flights at the airports, additional or better eating facilities are unlikely to provide external benefits to the airlines by stimulating many more passengers with local origins or destinations to use the airport. I believe these airport restaurants can influence the choices of transit passengers whether which country will be their transfer air plane's short journey staying airport destination to fly to their final destinations. Although, transit passengers usually stay to the transfer air plane airport in short time, but they hope that these any one transit staying airport can have any restaurants to provide good taste food to them to eat when they feel hungry, if the transfer air plane country's airport can provide enough restaurants and they can have different food taste choice and reasonable price. Then, the airport's restaurants may attract many short time transit passengers to choose to eat their food, even many passengers will like to choose the country's airline to buy tickets to stay short time to wait to transfer another air plane to fly to their final destination to replace another country's airport to stay short time.

Hence, it seems that any countries' airports' entertainment, eating and shopping service environment will influence any countries transit passengers whether they ought either choose to stay short time this country's airport in prefer or another country's airport to stay short time in prefer in order to decide to buy the country's airline air ticket for transfer airplane to another destination. Hence, any airports service environment will influence any countries passengers how to make transit airport destination short time staying choice.

However, I also suggest that an airport will place a lower revenue -over cost burden on that side of the travelling market that benefits the other the most. Assuming onc passenger

can earn benefit enjoyed by airlines from an extra-passenger using the airport, the airlines will be willing to pay up to this amount to increase passenger enjoyed benefit feeling.

The airport can extract rent from the airlines up to above their allocated costs for providing the airport short time staying platform (transfer air plane short time staying airport) for eating, entertainment, shopping need service of increasing their destination arriving passengers or transfer another air plane passengers number base. This involves transferring the external benefits derived by airlines from additional passengers using the transfer airport to the another destination airport.

On the another view, from a airport location choice perspective, locating or expanding an airport near a city center can reduce or at least contain passenger access costs . But, because land is like to be more expensive, the airside costs to airlines are serious higher and if the various other external costs of aviation are included. Hence, countryside or the airport is built far away from city center in the country. This location is one reasonable location choice, because it can reduce noise to influence people who are living when air planes are often flying or landing on the airport and the rent cost to the airport's any business renters will be influenced to reduce. Then, their food , product or entertainment service prices charge to the airport consumers will also be reduced. Thus, any airports ought nor neglect their building location choices in any countries because they will influence airport business renters sale prices.

THREE

Lean Maintenance Repair and Manual Error Airport Avoids Accident Service Occurrence Demand

Does any country airport's manual error accident

occurrence (airport staying traveller individual safety demand when he/she is staying in the country airport) influence overseas travellers their travelling destination choice in preference and transfer air plane country choice in preference ? Any airlines must need air plans to catch passengers to fly to travel. So, any air plans will need often to fly. Every flight will need long time to fly, e.g. short trip needs to fly less than five hours, even long trip needs to fly more than five hours, even ten hours. If many passengers choose the country to travel, the air plan needs to fly frequently to catch every flight passengers to go to the travelling destination frequently. So, any airlines air plans often need to check whether they have any engine machines has broken, need to be repaired in possible in order to let passengers feel the airline air plans are safe. If the airline's any air plans have occurred any accidents when they are flying, even the accidents cause any one passengers hurt, even death. Then, these flying accidents will let passengers feel life risk to choose this airline's any air plans to catch to fly. IN special, long time trip(s) flight(s). So, lean maintenance and engine check is needed to consider for any one airplane to any airline in order to improve efficiencies and minimize costs, maintenance, repair,

and overhaul services in the aviation industry sector, even avoiding any flying accident occurrence or reducing serious flying accidents occurrence chance to bring any one passenger

hurt, even death when they are catching any one of the airline air plans to travel. Thus, any one of airline safety is one important successful factor to any airlines.

Instead of passenger safety aspect, the flying logistics safety factor is also important. The central tenet of the lean

to a flying process can mainfest in a variety of ways , as over stalled
and underused inventory and misallocated labour, time transportation and logistics. From a customer's perspective, value-added activities are necessary and customers are willing to pay for activities(Bamber, 2000, Glass, 2016). For example, improvements caused by lean introduction in aviation industry in order to avoid misallocated labour time, increasing number of old broken tools, and obsolute jigs and fixtures. Aviation MRO services have been reported by the MIT Lean Aerospace Initiative (2005) to result in:

(1) Set up time: 17 to 85 percent improvement.
(2) Lead time: 16 to 50 percent improvement.
(3) Labour hours: 10 to 71 percent improvement.
(4) Cost: 11 to 50 percent improvement.
(5) Productivity: 27 to 100 percent improvement.
(6) Cycle time: 20 to 97 percent improvement.
(7) Airline airplane manufacturing factory floor space: 25 to 81 percent improvement.
(8) Travel distance (people and products): 42 to 95 percent improvement.
(9) Airplanes engine inventory or work in progress: 31 to 98 percent improvement.
(10) Scape, rework , deflects or inspection: 20 to 80 percent improvement.

Hence, any airlines' airplanes need to be achieve any one of above improvement at least percent level in order to keep airplane's accident occurrence chance to the least level. Moreover, airplanes' pilot employees their flying experiences or flight numbers factor is also important to influence airplane safe flying issue. Because if the pilot has less flying
expereince or he is not proficient pilot, or his flight number

is less. This pilot's individual flying factor will also influence the airplan's safety when he is driving the airplane.

So, any airlines need to consider how to train any one of pilot to be one proficient pilot, because id less experienced pilot , he/she is not proficient to drive any one airplane to fly. Then, the flying accident occurrence chance will also raise. It is one critical successful factor to influence passengers' confidence to choose the airline's airplanes to catch, instead of maintenance repair and checking engines factor.

On conclusion, raising travelling passengers' safe confidences factor will be one critical successful factor to influence any airlines' services level, because flying safety issue must be one important matter to be considered to any passengers when they decide to choose the airline's airplane to catch to fly to any destinations. If one airline can not guarantee any flying accidents won't occur, to cause any passengers hurt or death. Then, any passengers won't have confidence to feel its others services level can satisfy their basic flying enjoyment needs. Due to passengers' life cost must be no worth calculation more than other service cost. When they choose to catch the airlines' any one airplane to fly to the another destination form the country's airport. Hence, the influence of human factor in airport maintenance factor will influence any airlines' services feeling level to their passengers because human factor is one of the safety barrier which is used in order to prevent accidents or incidents of aircraft.

Therefore, the question is to which extent the error caused by human factor is included into the share of errors that are made during aircraft maintenance, such as flying accidents, incidents, injuries, death, damages related to

aircraft operation and maintenance. More airlines' detailed analyses have led to the knowledge that it is necessary to study the
interrelation of repair people, machines, airline factory maintenance and manufacturing working environment, and the air planes production processes. Human is the key factor production process and in the process of operation of technical means since gives new value to the object of any one airplane manufacturing process.

As a factor, the human is not perfect and introduces unintentional error in the system. It is important to develop a system of ever identification and to work constantly on error prevention. The works and activities on aircraft maintenance can produce hidden and active errors on the aircraft. Hidden errors are a type of errors that are seemingly invisible during aircraft
flying. Active errors are errors that occur immediately and result in immediate aircraft damage or injury , even death to any travelling passengers.

Hence, non human or without human factors will be less number to compare human factors to cause any flying incidents or accidents occurrence easily, e.g. damaging engine, old engine (no renew engine), fire, crash etc. different kinds of causes. However, the main causes of human errors to cause any flying accidents may include: lack of communication between the pilot(s)
and airport airplane landing staffs, complacency (assessment of work according to previous working experience), lacking of flying knowledge to the pilot, distraction, lack of team work, fatigue, lack of materials and technological support), pressure on the work performer, lack of assertiveness (lack of self-confidence or technical approach to work),stress (working under

pressure), lack of awareness etc. different human factors. Any one of above human factors will influence any flying accidents cause.

Moreover, instead of human factor, the flying working environment which refers to the space and place for work as well as the conditions of work factor will also influence human error occurrence increasing chance, e.g. time pressure, equipment and tools enough number supplies, night shift, all of any one work environment factor will also influence human error occurrence increasing chance in any flight flying. However, the factors that lead to cause of maintenance error may be caused from wrong information system supplies of equipment , aircraft manufacturer, wrong working equipment and tools, wrong design of aircraft equipment and parts, incorrect working task arrangement, lacking technical education to the aircraft maintenance workers, employee's bad personality, poor aircraft factory manufacturing working environment, poor airline company organization structure, working management and control and poor communication etc. different manual or non manual factors.

Hence, all of above any one non manual factors will also raise manual error factor to cause any flying accidents occurrence chances. However, if any airlines hope to satisfy their passengers' flying service level. They must consider non manual and manual both factors for aircraft lean maintenance repair service aspect.

● Influence of airside and off airport service facility to the country airport geographical choice (travellers' airport service facility demand to the country airport)

What does airport airside means ? It includes a system of three components: runways, taxiways and agron-gate areas, on which aircraft and aircraft support vehicles operate. It brings this questions: Why can airport airside operation influence passengers feeling to the country's airport and airline services? How does it influence airport ground service staffs' service performance?

In fact, this airside airport physical area choice has direct relationship between aircraft and apron gate areas of the terminal processing of passenger and cargo. They are major factors to influence operations on runway component. It means that airport ground service staffs' service efficiency, used for the passengers and air fright catching any airplanes processing.

Hence, in a geographical sense, landside and airside capacity on how designing and building og geographical area can bring indirect influence to passengers. They need to enter or indirect influence the airport , in special, many flights are staying on the airport runway as well as many passengers need to leave from the airplanes or enter to the airplanes in the same time on the airport boundary. Hence, if the airport has good airside design , then many passengers will feel convenient to leave or enter the airport from the airside areas.

Airports are perhaps truly intermodel terminals in the transportatoin system. They provide an intersafe among air highway, rail and even water way travel. They are an important part of the medium and long distance intercity transportation system in our future transportation tools. Hence, it has enough reasons to support airside geographical airside and off airport factors can influence an airport and its airline flying service providers on its capacity as well as how it's capacity can influence passengers' satisfactory level when they arrive the country's airport. Hence, airport's congestion growth problem that is needed to consider to any airports because when one airport 's congestion is growing.

It will influence passengers service satisfactory level to be fallen down in possible, e.g. capacity is increased by the addition of a new access road, such as additions provide a major increase. Thus, the stair step growth, it will cause congestion growth because if the airport had used many areas for stair step growth and passengers will have less space to let them to walk on the ground and their airport congestion feeling will also increase when passengers are staying to leave the airport or waiting for check in or check out or waiting to transfer another airplane in the country's airport

The major airside factors to influence travelling passengers whose airport service feeling may include as below:

Availability of enough land for expansion for runways, availability of aids to navigation and air traffic control techniques that could result in reduction of separation between aircraft , noise, aircraft mix, load factor, exclusive use and use of gates , enough airside and outside facilities, availability of airspace, whether aircraft large size is enough capacity and where is location of gates, staffing, equipment freight, environmental protection regulation, and community attitudes toward airside operation.

Thus, whether the airport has enough facilities to satisfy passengers staying in its airport service need, it will have indirect influence further passengers increasing or decreasing number problem. For example, if the airport terminal functions are spread over a large geographic area, access and facilities have to be expanded to accommodate the spread-out configuration of the terminal or if terminal facilities are grouped together, the access facilities can be congregated into a smaller geographical area.

The capacity of the landside is a function of the terminal design , which has a major influence on the relative to between airside and landside capacity. Also, these off airport factors can also
influence landside capacity, they may include: off airport parking, off airport terminals, urban development pattern, multiple jurisdiction, financial resources etc. issues. The sub factors of the off-airport access functions , they can influence passengers' services feeling to the airport. They may include: user and vehicle characteristics, e.g. occupants per vehicle, separate and preferential guide way subsystems, roadway traffic management, access link to major transportation , transportation connections. All of these airside and off-airport facilities will
influence passengers' servicing feeling when they arrive any countries' airports. Hence, any countries' airports ought not neglect any one of these minor airside facilities of inside airports to outside airports both.

The another geographical choice airport building issue, it is also one critical factor for how the development of airport cities. It will influence passengers' service feeling to any country airport. The questions may include: Why may any country need to develop an airport city? Can it bring economic benefit and attract many passengers to choose to travel the country? Can the airport city reform to raise airport service performance or service level? Airports have become new dynamic centers of economic activity, incorporating several commercial and entertainment services inside passenger terminals, when developing a hotels and accommodations , office complexes, conference and exhibition centers or leisure facilities choices for leisure passengers and business passengers both.

Airport-centered development may occur at different spatial scales (from the micro scale of the passenger terminal to the regional or metropolitan scale), thus assuming different shapes and mainfestations. Different concepts to address these developments can be found in the " airport city", airport corridor, and aerotopolis (Guller, M. & Guller, M, 2003).

I shall explain how airport city concept can help to raise passenger service performance feeling in airports and airlines as below:

In general, airport passengers hope airports ought provide these different kinds service and achievement the lowest satisfactory service quality or performance level to let them to feel, such as air transport needs have complex airport -neighborhood interactions (in what concerns an eventual development towards the concept of airport city) requires the identification of thes takeholders involved and an awareness of the relationships between them. Any airport's main task needs to provide traveling, air transport, shipping, entertainment services to the dual market of airlines and travelers. As such, its primary interaction consists of the supply and demand relationship with the users stakeholder group (passengers and airlines), which results in broad terms in the airports aeronautical revenues. Furthermore, non-aeronautical (commercial) revenues also result from the interactions between airport and users, namely from agents such as cargo and passengers oriented organizations who pay rents or concession feeling to the airport authority, depending on the commercial arrangements binding these agents.

Thus, one successful airport city, it ought provide good neighborhood transport service to travelling passengers, e.g. bus, taxi, ferry etc. public transportation service. It aims to avail any airport passengers can catch any one of these public transportation tools to arrive airport or leave the airport easily. It also needs to provide hotel, conference service for business visitors as well as retail shops, cinemas for shopping visitors or entertainment visitors when they are staying in the country's airport(s). Also, it ought provide facilities to any cargo -oriented
organizations to deliver any cargo in short time rapidly. So, one airport's any neighborhood facilities have relationship to influence any passengers and airport organizations' service performance feeling between different user agents including: service provision (e.g. between passengers and businesses), business transactions, supply and demand (e.g. between public transport providers and passengers and passengers or visitors) and employer-employee relationships (businesses and workforce , such as airport airline ground service workers). Because if they feel that they can work in one comfortable airport working environment, they will feel happy and enjoyable to serve their passengers more everyday. It means that any airports' facilities will have indirect relationship to influence airport ground service workers' psychology to feel either enjoyable or hate to work in the airport environment often.

On conclusion, airports ought need to consider themselves airside and off airport facilities whether they have enough supplies and innovate their facilities to be better , even perfect in order to satisfy any airport visitors, travelers, user organizations and airport ground service employees to enjoy to work and use their services if they hope their service level or performance is satisfied to their service needs for long term.

FOUR

INFLUENCING AIR CONNECTIVITY TO AIRPORT ENVIRONMENT SERVICE QUALITY DEMAND

Can air connectivity growth decreases travel costs for attracting travelling passengers, consumers and businesses and facilities global productive growth? Can the country aiport environment service quality influence its transfer air plane traveller preference choice and travelling destination preference choice ? This seems to be particularly an issue when airport capacity is scare or when new airports are added to an existing airport system. What is air connectivity ? Why does air connectivity raise passengers services? How to measure air connective service?

When direct and indirect connectivity relate to the airport connectivity available to local travelling passengers, any airports ought need to raise extra airline services to raise service quality , e.g. cheaper air ticket price, in-flight service extra service provision, e.g. comfortable and clean and quiet air port waiting environment

service provision and feeling. However, passengers will generally prefer direct, non-stop connections over indirect air connectivity service.

Air connectivity service can assist airlines to raise competitive effort an offer and they provide access to the many destinations with too little demand for a direct flight, such as minimum connecting time differs in quality , due to in-flight time differences, the inconvenience and risk of missing a connection and transfer time for direct or indirect flights. Hence, any airlines can reduce passengers indirect or direct flight in-flight time to wait airplanes arrive to catch when they arrive any airports. This air inflight

waiting time shorten service will attract many passengers to choose the airline to catch airplanes if its inflight waiting time to airport passengers is lesser than other airlines‘ in-flight waiting time in any airports. It can raise airline service quality, due to the airline has many passengers feel in-flight waiting time is shorten than other airlines often.

In fact, airport connectivity is one good concept method to raise passengers' satisfactory service level. One of the important factors for the connectivity of airports may include: The size

and economic strength of the local catchment area how drives outbound demand, size and economic activities as well as tourism attractiveness are an important cariable

factor in explaining
inbound demand (including the propensity to flying demand), landside accessibility drives the size of the catchment area that airlines can serve from a particular airport within a certain landside travel time, apart from the socio-economic variables factor, also cultural , political and the historical ties play a role in explaining demand the origin-destination level factor. All of the research on the factors that explain air level, demand at the origin-destination or airport level is widespread, including gravity modelling (e.g. a bed at al., 2001) and regressions on aggregate
airport demand (Dobruszkes, 2011). All of any one factors may be airport connectivity service to influence passengers' service feeling level in airports and airlines both service quality.

ON airport visit costs aspect, airlines also need to consider airport visit costs in their route development strategy. Visit costs may also influence passenger choice behavior when
airlines pass on higher/lower charges to the passenger through air fares. Although, airport visit costs generally represent a limited share of an airline's total operational costs, this share can be more significant for short haul flights as well as fair airlines. All of any one these airport charges and passenger fees variable may influence passengers airlines choice. They may include:

Fees variable, landing charge, parking charge for their vehicles or aircraft, passenger luggage charge, security charge, boarding bridge charge, noise charge, emission charge, airport development service increasing charge, check -in charge, terminal charge, cargo charge. So, if any one of these charges influence the airline ticket price rises, it will influence passengers' air ticket purchase choice to the airline in possible.

On airport service levels aspect, for keeping and attracting passengers, airlines and airports need to compete with services that improve the passengers experience. Such service

factors concern for immigration and luggage, but also relate to the terminals, waiting transfer another air plane time, shopping facilities, toilets, atmosphere and space cleaniness, friendliness of staff and availability of delicated lounges. Together they determine the image of an airport and its perceived value by passengers and airlines.

On airline routes development aspect, it can also influence passengers choices to the airline, e.g. Australia airline had developed long route to England destination. Any Australia passengers can fly to England route directly. They do not need to transfer another air plane to go to England. Although, flying time is above 12 hours long time, but it can bring available to passengers. They do not need to spend time to wait another air plane to transfer to go England in Australia any airports. THus, airline route development strategy airline planners require detailed, accurate information to make new route decisions, but airlines usually do not have the resources to fully evaluate every new route market. So, they need a sound well articulated business case, can convince airlines to introduce new air services, as well as airport / destinations can influence the airline planning process.

For example, Interviewer indicates that new routes are a huge investment and risk to an airline in airline economic view point, if the airline had not gathered any data to evaluate whether the new route is worth to develop and predict passengers' new route choice behavior. It assumed

75% lead factor will influence any new route development in success. It indicates these different aircraft type and seats per flight, annual passenger requirements data for these aircrafts: Boeing 747 aircraft needs to satisfy 400 at least seats per flight and annual passenger requirement need 219, 000, aircraft airbus A340 aircraft needs 280 at least seats per flight and annual passenger requirements need 153,300 , Boesing 767 to 300 aircraft needs 220 at least seats per flight and annual passenger requirements need 120, 450 . Boeing 737 to 700 aircraft needs 76,650 and regional Jet aircraft needs 100 at least seats per flight and annual passenger requirements need 54,750.

Hence, any airlines need have route priorities strategy before they decide which new flight route(s) will be developed , in order to achieve airlines add service in order of expected profitability, different airlines have pursued different strategies, destinations can move up the priority board with: solid research and analysis (always) and incentives (sometimes).However, any airline questions for new routes may include as below:

What is the current, actual market for a potential route?
How much can my airline stimulate the flight flying market?
How will the competition react?
How much market share will achieve?
How will be the connectivity contribution?
Will the new route be a financial success?

Hence, any airlines need to reduce uncertainty and risk, before they decide to develop any new route market.

The air service development process may include as below:

Step one: market assessment, required a quantify the time size of the existing air travel market step two: strategy, deficiency analysis and detailed route analysis

step three: business case analysis, packaging and presenting the information to airlines

step fourth: evaluate and negotiate airline incentives

It is the final steps an appropriate incentive, in certain circumstances, helps airlines commit to new air service to satisfy any new route passengers' more satisfactory flying needs.

Similarly, the strategy steps follow: benchmark air services, identify deficiencies, identify new route opportunities, identify potential air service providers, assess viability of potential air services and prioritize route opportunities and target carriers.

Any airlines may find any information concerns new route business cases to decide their countries flying new routes choice , such as: catchment area profile: demographics, economy, tourist etc. information, airport profile : traffic and facilities information market profile; market sizes , top city pairs, traffic leakage etc. information, suggested service : frequency , schedule, airport routing information, route analysis: market share, load factor, stimulation potential, self-diversion etc. information, any airlines' past flying routes strategic considerations etc. information in order to predict and evaluate whether how many further passenger number is flying that they accept to choose the new flying routes travelling needs.

Hence, how to design to impact either the supply or demand for any new flight routes that is only important because of the country has less number of passengers accept to choose the new flying route to fly. Then, the new flying route does not needed to be design to supply to the country's travelling passengers because their acceptance to this new flying route ends are very less. However, the demand level is low new flying route needs to satisfy these three qualifying services criteria, such as: Are new routes only? Increase on existing routes? Does it work service rent incentives? Will the new flying route be satisfied to air service to the airline passengers and airport waiting passengers, e.g. strategically important? Marginally (unprofitable) self-sustaining in the short term? New flying routes only? Increase an existing routes? Service rent incentives?

How can airports afford aggressive airline incentive / fee discounts and still fund route development marketing in a difficult economy? I recommend that the solution method may include new flying route design and developing and maximizing non-aeronautical revenue streams both, such as retail and duty free, food and beverage, parking , loyalty and premium programs and land development to airport building. Marketing funding strategy may be an ineffective incentive for travelling destinations. However, it may not differentiate a market, as route marketing incentives are used by over 80% of communities in the U.S. marketing incentives can be: Unilateral airport pays 100% or cooperative airlines matches some portion, funding amounts are often tied on the capacity of inbound seats to be available on the new flight (flying) route. By calculating the economic impact of new visitors (spend at the destination), a destination can calculate the return on investment in cooperative new flight (flying) route market.

On conclusion, air connectivity is one important factor to influence any country's travelling passengers to the airline's service quality or service level in order to achieve new flying (flight) route design , reducing inflight transfer another airplane waiting time in airport, or marketing development in success. So, any airlines can not neglect this air connectivity will influence their passengers' service quality.Hence, air connectivity factor is also very important to influence any travelling passengers' service satisfactory level.

- How to measure and rise airline
service performance to achieve traveller individual service demand level

How are airline performing ? Nowadays, the rise of the low cost airlines' competition is serious, due to airlines hope to rise themselves attractions to influence passengers to choose to use their travelling services. So, different airlines have spend long time to build their unique person-to-person passenger services, which passengers use of different airlines, e.g. digital electronic air tickets purchase method. Any airlines hope to make each journey personalized to the individual will gain market share and improve its service quality to be more unique in order to reach the efforts of airlines to build high levels of customer service appears to have been generally noticed by passengers, when they choose to buy the airline's digital electronic ticket or paper air ticket to use its flying service.

Hence, improvement their digital e-ticket purchase experience and communications factor, for example, if any passengers can enter the airline's air ticket purchase website to buy electronic ticket to pre-book seats in the short time rapidly as well as there are enough seats number to supply to them to pre-book. So, they do not need to worry about without any seats to supply to them to catch the airline's flight to fly to anywhere in any time available conveniently. So, it seems that there is plenty of space for airlines to grow and improve their digital experience and communication method to let any passengers to feel, if the airline hopes to let its passengers to feel that it has unique service to compare others airlines.

The aviation industry plays a major role in the aspect of work and leisure to passengers around the global. So, nowadays passengers‘ demands to any airlines’ service quality had been raised. Hence, any airline service industry messengers are under pressure to prove their services are customers oriented service improvement of performance that guarantees competitive advantages to the global travelling marketplace. So, it also implies that any airlines‘ services performance will be influenced to cause many passengers feel more poor and let passengers dissatisfy the airline’s service performance. The, the airline will possible lose many passengers, due to passengers have many airlines choices, they can find any airlines to replace which any one airline to buy air ticket from internet at home immediately.

However, airlines’ comfortable seats arrangement service provision feeling factor is still important in preferable to compare other factors, because passengers must need to sit any seats in any air planes. So, whether the air plane can provide new comfortable seats to let passengers to feel this factor is still the most important factor to influence any passengers to choose to the airline’s air plane to catch. For example, service comfortability is how passengers observed the quality of service offered them by the airline’s cleanliness, quiet zone, shops, restaurants and business pavilion in functioning like staffs, information desk, and in flight announcement are included as tangible features by the passengers (Geraldine et a.,2013). All of these factors are needed often to measure whether their service performances are satisfactory to themselves passengers service needs.

Moreover, the other factors may include service affordability , it can be regarded as given passenger the opportunity to select from inclusive air ticket prices made available to the different group of passengers by the airlines, as a gesture of goodwill , to establish and reinforce customer loyalty and repeat purchases essential for the airline continuity as well as service reliability. it is the probability that airline will carry out its expected function satisfactory as stated in the flight schedule. Hence, there is a strong link between different airlines' service quality variables, airline image and repeat patronage from the passengers.

Service quality is a measure of how well the service level delivered matches passengers expectations to measure service quality based on input from focus groups. It consists of five factors (tangibles, reliability, responsiveness, assurance and empathy). All of these factors will be identifies that how the airline service quality can be satisfactory to its passengers ' psychological and emotion enjoyable service needs.

Any one of these any five service factors will be important to influence the airline's passengers service feeling level to the airline. It means that the passenger will have more chance to choose the airline's service again (repeating purchase its air ticket). Hence, any airlines can not neglect any one of service feeling to its passengers. It needs often to enquire questionnaires to evaluate whether its these five aspects of service quality , if it discovered any of these five aspects of service level is poor, e.g. 5 scale is the best service performance level, then it can attempt to find its error whether which aspects, it needs to very need to reach the 5 scale , the best service performance level when many passengers feel, e.g. enquiring 100 passengers who give 5 scale to reliability service aspect, before reliability service aspect has less than 50% passengers from 100 passengers who feel the airlines concerns this reliable service level aspect questions to be the best. It is one kind of measurement service quality method to any airlines.

Other service performance evaluation factor is satisfaction in the job to every airline front service or ground service staffs to the airline. Job satisfaction describes how content an employee is with his or her job. It is how the employee responses to a job. It can be considered as a part of life satisfaction to one organization, when the employee is working in the organization. Hence, if one airline front service as ground service staff who can feel more job satisfaction to compare his/her prior airline employer. Then, he/she won't be easy to change his/her present airline employer.

However, some factors can influence job satisfaction are pay and benefit, fair performance appraisal, career and promotional opportunities, proper reward and recognition, work-family life balance, the job itself, proper working conditions, leadership chance, autonomy in work.

Job satisfaction can also involve complex number of variables, circumstances, opinions and behavioral tendencies and a variety of work related outcomes, such as commitment, involvement, motivation, satisfaction, attendance. Hence, any airlines also need to concern how let their employees feel job satisfaction issue in order to avoid their leaving turnover number increases, due to job satisfaction and dissatisfaction depend on the expectations what the job supplies for an employee not the nature of the job.

Finally, instead of concerning employees job satisfaction issue, any airlines also need to concern passengers satisfaction issue because it will have any passengers will choose the airline, if it can bring more service satisfaction to let them to feel , then they will become repeat passengers to the airline.

What kinds of factors passengers were looking for and what were the reasons of choosing a specific airline? When one airline often is complained from its passengers. It will have more mistakes to let them to feel or dissatisfy its service. Hence the airlines needs to find which are its mistakes and improve in order to satisfy its passengers' expectations, e.g. finding what are the mistakes to the airlines' serious concern regarding passenger complaints and complaint satisfaction in order to make the airline more likely to meet its passengers' expectation in case of a problem. Hence, any airlines need to concern how to improve its employees' satisfactory service as well as its passengers' satisfactory service both issues as well as how to measure their service quality whether is enough to achieve general service acceptable performance to its passengers.

Reference

A bed, S. Y. A.O. Ba-Fail and S.M. Jasimuddin (2001), " An economatic analysis of international air travel demand in Saudi Arabia". Journal of air transport managmement, vol. 7, pp.143-148.

Bamber, L., & Dale, B.G. Lean production : a study of application in a traditoinal manufacturing environment. Production planning & control, 11 (3), 291-298, 2000.

Dobruszkes, F.M. Lennert and G. Van Hamme (2011). " An analysis of the determinants of air traffic volume for European metropolitan area". Journal of transport geographyy, vol. 19/4/pp.755-762.

Gealdine, O., & David , U.C. (2013). effects of airline service quality on airline image and passengers' loyalty: Findings from Arill Air Nigeria passengers, Journal of hospitality and management tourism, 4(2), 19-28. doi: http://dx.doi: 10.5897/HMT 2013, 0089.

Glass, R., Seifermann, S., & Metternich, J. The spread of lean production in the assembly, Process and maching industry. Procedia CIRP, 55, 278-283, 2016.

Guller, M. & Guller, M. (2003) From Airport to airport city. Editional Gustavo , Gili, Barcel on a.

Intervistas Consulting Inc. Massachusetts Institute Of Technology (MIT), Lean Aerospace Initiative, Available: www.lean.mit.edu, 2005.

9 798887 497174

Printed by Libri Plureos GmbH in Hamburg,
Germany